S. R. Howarth

PRUNING

THIS Book has been specially
written by Mr. Roy Genders to
cover the requirements of the gardener and allotment holder.

It deals with every aspect of
pruning all types of fruit trees
and bushes, shrubs, roses, etc.

General Editor: W. A. FOYLE

4s

PRUNING

BY

ROY GENDERS

W. & G. FOYLE LTD.
119-125, CHARING CROSS ROAD, LONDON, W.C.2.

First published 1955
Reprinted 1956
Reprinted 1962

© *W. & G. Foyle Ltd., 1958*

PRINTED AND BOUND IN
GREAT BRITAIN BY
THE HOLLEN STREET PRESS LTD
LONDON, W.1

CONTENTS

CHAPTER   PAGE

I.   WHY PRUNE AT ALL?
Why do we Prune — Study each variety —
When to Prune — Root Pruning — Results of
Pruning — Functions of Roots and foliage —
Timing the Crop — Bark Ringing   9

II.   TOOL REQUIREMENTS
Need for efficient tools — Care in selecting tools
— Efficient Secateurs — Use of the Saw — Shears
and their uses — The pruning knife — Making
the correct cut   15

III.   PRUNING ROSES
Hard v. Light Pruning — Study each variety —
When to Prune — Moderate Pruning — Planting
and Pruning new trees — Standard Roses —
Suckers — Pruning for Successional flowering —
Weeping Standards — Correct way to Prune —
Roses indoors   20

IV.   CLIMBING AND WALL PLANTS
Climbers requiring different pruning technique
— Ceanothus — Clematis — Coronilla glauca
— Cydonia Japonica — Elaeagnus — Garrya
elliptica — Honeysuckle — Hydrangea petiolaris
— Ivy — Jasmine — Magnolia — Myrtle —
Pyracantha — Roses — Vines — Wisteria   ...   27

V.   FLOWERING SHRUBS
The need for Pruning Shrubs — Acer — Arbutus
— Azalea — Berberis — Buddleia — Chimonan-
thus fragrans — Cornus — Cotoneaster —
Cytisus — Daphne — Deutzia — Escallonia —
Forsythia — Fuchsia — Hamamelis — Hibiscus
— Hydrangea — Kerria — Lavender — Lilac —
Osmarea — Philadelphus — Rhododendron —
Ribes — Rose — Rosemary — Santolina —
Senecio — Syringa — Veronica — Viburnum —
Weigela   33

VI.   PRUNING ORNAMENTAL TREES
Renovating neglected trees — Pruning specimen
trees — Conifers — Individual treatment of
ornamental trees — Acer — Almond — Ash
— Beech — Birch — Cerasus — Chestnut —
Crataegus — Davidia — Elm — Hornbeam —
Laburnum — Mulberry — Oak — Poplar —
Prunus — Pyrus — Sorbus — Walnut — Willow   39

VII. CARE AND PRUNING OF HEDGES AND WINDBREAKS
Different pruning treatment for different plants
— Arbutus — Beech — Berberis stenophylla —
Birch — Box — Buddleia — Conifers — Coton-
easter Franchetti — Escallonia — Gorse — Hazel
— Holly — Hornbeam — Hydrangea — Laurel
— Lonicera — Olearia — Pear — Pittosporum
Mayi — Privet — Pyracantha — Rose —
Tamarix — Thuya plicata — Whitehorn — Yew   45

VIII. RENOVATING OLD FRUIT TREES. APPLES AND PEARS
Cutting out dead wood — Pruning young trees
— Restricting the vigorous tree — Bark Pruning   51

IX.   CARE OF A YOUNG FRUIT TREE. APPLES AND PEARS
Building the framework — The established Spur
System — The Regulated System — The
Renewal System — Biennial Cropping — Branch
Bending — Notching and Nicking   57

X.   TRAINING YOUNG TREES. APPLES AND PEARS
Value of trained Trees — Bush and Standard
Forms — Dwarf Pyramids — Cordons — Hori-
zontal form.   64

XI.   TREATMENT AND PRUNING OF STONE FRUITS
Plums — Spring Pruning — Root Pruning —
Treatment of the Fan trained tree — Forming the
Fan Shaped Tree — Cherries — Morello cherries
— Peaches and Nectarines — Apricots   70

XII. PRUNING THE VINE AND FIG
The Vine — Alternative Pruning Methods —
Growing Indoors — The Long Rod System —
The Spur System — Outdoor Cultivation —
Figs — Pruning for Fruit — Root Pruning   ...   75

XIII. PRUNING AND TRAINING SOFT FRUITS
Pruning to lengthen the life of a fruiting bush —
Black Currants — Red Currants — The Goose-
berry — Raspberries — The Loganberry — The
Blackberry and Hybrid Berries — Japanese Wine-
berry 81

INDEX 87

CHAPTER I

WHY PRUNE AT ALL?

Why do we Prune — Study each variety — When to Prune —
Root Pruning — Results of Pruning — Functions of Roots and
foliage — Timing the Crop — Bark Ringing.

OF all jobs in the garden nothing causes so much controversy as
does pruning and nothing causes so much worry. We hear it
said that one's roses should be pruned and so should the fruit
trees at the required time, but we rarely give a thought to why
they should be pruned, or to how it should be done, and the
correct time seems to matter little. As long as we can obtain a
good pair of pruners, the plants are generally hacked about at
will and without the least bit of law and order. I have never
forgotten the time when my father called in a respectable firm of
nurserymen to tidy up his garden and the look on his face when
he saw that a massive white lilac, his pride and joy in early
summer, which always covered itself with a mass of bloom, had
been hacked back to just the main stem. 'Butchered' would be a
better word, for it never recovered from the shock and never
again carried more than an odd bloom in June. Any old tree,
so severely pruned will generally succumb and the same way that
an old man losing both legs will surely die whereas a young person
would most often withstand the shock. A young rose tree just
planted should be pruned hard, whereas an old neglected tree
must only gradually be brought back to renewed vigour. But
few ever ask themselves exactly why pruning is done. Why not
just let the trees and bushes run wild just as they used to do in the
cottage gardens of old?

WHY DO WE PRUNE?

Pruning is done for a number of reasons.

(a) It may be required to grow blooms for exhibition or of
like quality for one's enjoyment in garden or home and
only by sustaining the vigour of a plant, can it be expected
to produce a bloom of top quality. To allow the plant
to run more or less wild will mean that it will produce a
large number of poor quality blooms that will become
smaller and smaller.

(b) Then it may be necessary to prune in the case of fruiting
trees and bushes, not only to train them to the required
size and shape but so that they will give the largest amount

9

of quality fruit in the smallest possible area and in the quickest possible time.

(c) Again, in the case of shrubs, it will be necessary to constantly cut away all unwanted wood and to keep the plants under control. The removal of unwanted wood will mean that more new wood is made and this is the vigorous wood and so it will be necessary to train the plant into the required shape and especially if the garden is small, to keep it to its allotted area. A strong growing shrub allowed to grow at will may quickly crowd its more dainty neighbours out of existence.

(d) Also, the question of pruning covers the subject of disease. The removal of all decayed or ill-formed branches or shoots will help to keep the tree healthy and ensure that it will divert its strength to only the healthy wood.

(e) And lastly, pruning is done to ensure that the maximum of air and sunlight is able to reach all parts, and particularly the centre of a tree or bush, not only to ripen the wood and keep it healthy but also to ensure the complete ripening of the fruit or the maturity of the bloom.

Thus in a nutshell, pruning ensures vigour, correct shape and quality and it is essential to realise just why we prune before a pair of pruners are ever taken into the hand.

STUDY EACH VARIETY

It is not a question of pruning for pruning's sake just because your next door neighbour prunes or the gardening periodicals tell us to. First, decide why your fruit trees and roses and soft fruit bushes require pruning and then go ahead at the correct time, but only after studying the requirements of each variety on its merits. For instance, with fruit trees, the tip bearers, those which bear their fruits on the new lateral wood rather than on the spurs, require very different treatment than do the spur bearers. Also the question of training the trees will be quite different, for the tip bearers do not make suitable trees when trained as cordons or horizontals, or in any artificial form.

With roses, certain varieties require only moderately light pruning whilst others respond to more vigorous cutting back. But do not make the mistake of cutting back your new rose bushes to the base as a friend of mine did recently. Only the best of the new varieties had been purchased and in my friend's enthusiasm to obtain exhibition quality blooms, he had cut them

back to ground level, to the scion, with the result that the following year he had nothing but suckers.

The very wide range of shrubs demands detailed knowledge
of their individual habits. Some respond to much more severe
pruning than others. For instance, the buddleias will stand quite
severe cutting back and will come again the following year with
increased vigour. Not so the lilacs which I prefer to leave entirely
alone except for the removal of dead wood.

Reverting to top fruits, the cherries and plums should not
receive anything like the pruning as performed on either pears
or apples chiefly because of their habit of 'bleeding' which will
not only sap their strength if carried to extreme, but will make
the trees liable to disease entering through the wound.

WHEN TO PRUNE

This brings us to the question of the correct time to prune and
here again there are many variations. Generally speaking, those
trees which come into bloom late in the season will benefit from
spring pruning, whilst those flowering early in spring should be
pruned in autumn. For instance, the autumn fruiting raspberries
should be spring pruned; those fruiting in summer having their
decayed and excessive cane growth pruned out in autumn.

Black and red currants are generally placed under the same
heading and will most often be planted close to each other in the
garden, but they are plants with quite different habits and so
must be given different treatment with the pruners. Red currants
form lateral shoots from the main stem, whilst black currants
throw up the new wood from the base. Here the old wood needs
to be cut right out, but when dealing with red currants it is merely
a matter of cutting back to an inch of the main stem to form a
type of spur.

The question of frost must also come into general reckoning
and this means situation and district. It is unwise to do any
pruning on roses before mid-April in those gardens situated north
of a line drawn from Chester to Lincoln, for fear of frost damage.
Likewise many of the not quite hardy shrubs should be allowed
to retain their previous season's growth as protection, shrubs
like the fuchsia and hydrangea, both of which come late into
bloom and which will be happy with April pruning.

ROOT PRUNING

The more general methods of pruning consist of removing

an entire branch or shoot, or merely cutting back to a bud which may mean removing no more than an inch or two of wood. But there is another form of pruning and this is concerned with shortening the roots, or root pruning which is generally performed if the particular tree or plant suffers from injury caused by branch removal, such as the plum; or it may be done to restrict a vigorous variety like Blenheim Orange apple which would become even more vigorous if much wood was removed. Again, a tree may have been trained to a definite size or shape and any vigorous pruning would spoil it. Root pruning must therefore be done and particularly is this necessary when trying to restrict the growth of fan-shaped trees growing against a wall. The apple grower is helped in this direction by the dwarf stocks available for a restricted garden, but other fruits like peaches and cherries must rely on other methods of restriction of which root pruning is the safest method.

RESULTS OF PRUNING

But just because a rose bush will produce a larger bloom when pruned and make a bush of more robust habit, likewise an apple tree will bear a larger fruit, there must be a reason for it. Why does correct pruning bring about these results? By removing certain parts of a tree it will mean that what is left will receive a

PRUNING A NEW APPLE TREE

greater amount of the essential foods to promote healthy stem and foliage in the form of sap, air and light. The diagram will show more clearly what happens.

Let us suppose that this is a newly planted fruit tree, then for instance, the shoots B° and C are pruned where shown, it will mean that shoot A will receive extra sap and also more air and light, the vigour of the tree being directed to that particular shoot 'A'. But in order to bring the tree into quicker bearing it will be better to prune back shoot 'A' in a similar manner so that the tree will be able to concentrate its energies in producing fruit rather than on new growth. Thus the flow of sap is held in check. This also leads up to the question of pruning not only to produce an early crop and of top quality, but to the training of a tree to the required form which is dealt with in the appropriate chapters.

FUNCTIONS OF ROOTS AND FOLIAGE

Continually it must be borne in mind that there is close affinity between root growth and foliage. The roots supply the raw materials that are to be turned to good account by the foliage which in turn supplies other substances which are continually building up a more vigorous rooting system which in their turn are searching for more nourishment for the foliage to convert. By controlling either roots or foliage, this cycle is halted for a time, but it can be seen that too drastic pruning of either roots or foliage will have its effect in throwing the functions of the plant quite out of tune with one another. It is therefore necessary before doing any pruning to remember the close affinity between foliage and roots. If pruning is done at the wrong time of the year, it will cause severe harm to the functions of the plant. If roses for instance are pruned whilst the leaves are fulfilling their functions in mid-summer, the constitution of the plant will suffer; the roots will be searching out for nourishment which cannot be converted by the foliage. The result would be that soon the plant would die back altogether. Likewise any tree when in full foliage. A little judicious thinning to allow more light to enter may be in order or pinching back of surplus shoots of plums and other fruits, but any severe removal of foliage during the period the sap is most active will mean a tree of reduced vigour, rather than one of additional vigour if pruning is done whilst the sap is dormant. Throughout the life of a tree the aim must be kept constantly in mind, that it is required to first build up a vigorous tree; to ensure a bloom or fruit of top quality, and then to maintain a constant affinity between health, vigour and quality, all of which is not difficult if we realise just why it is necessary to prune before we take up the pruners.

TIMING THE CROP

Pruning also plays an important part in the question of timing. For instance when growing roses indoors it may be a more profitable business to have the main flush of flowers early in the New Year. This being the case, the plants will need to be prevented from flowering in autumn so that they may build up their strength for later flowering.

This may only be achieved if each new shoot is pruned back during early summer, to three buds, so that they can concentrate their energies into making growth for the New Year. In much the same way are the autumn fruiting raspberries pruned in early summer so that they will not make new growth too soon, for it is in September that they are required to fruit and not in mid-summer, as do other varieties.

In exactly the same way are the autumn fruiting strawberries de-blossomed until early May for their fruit is not required until the end of the season.

BARK RINGING

Besides summer and winter pruning of fruit trees and the method of pruning the roots, there is also another way of pruning or restricting and that is bark pruning or cutting which is done late in spring. This checks the flow of sap to the foliage and thus the strength of the tree is diverted to the formation of fruit buds rather than to making more foliage. This is only necessary where a tree may be making too much new wood and bearing very little fruit.

But before embarking on any of these pruning operations, stop to consider the need for pruning. Why is it necessary to prune a given tree other than to prune for pruning's sake? It must first be understood the reasons for commencing operations which will be one or more of those we have discussed. Then look at the subject for some little time before commencing operations, for remember that many a branch has been removed from a tree or bush in haste which immediately after has been regretted. It may be necessary to go over the same tree on a number of occasions, removing just the right amount of wood which will provide light and air, or removing the right growth so that the remainder may grow on to the required shape or size. Study each variety; in rose trees it is most often found that the white varieties, being more vigorous than the others, will require cutting back more severely. Likewise the buddleia Charming, a new pale pink variety, should not be cut back as vigorously as Royal Red. Study each tree or variety entirely on its merits after having decided if pruning is necessary and then proceed carefully and with intelligence. To cut away, like a poor barber, without any plan will only cause disappointment.

CHAPTER II

TOOL REQUIREMENTS

Need for efficient tools — Care in selecting tools — Efficient
Secateurs — Use of the saw — Shears and their uses — The
pruning knife — Making the correct cut.

To be able to prune properly one must be in possession of the necessary tools, tools which will give the correct cut without causing bruising or tearing. A cut badly made, particularly if close to a bud, may become a source of disease, or the bud itself may be seriously harmed and it must be remembered that most of the wood which is to be pruned will be fairly hard and in some instances really tough. It is therefore essential that the tool should be capable of dealing with the particular wood in the cleanest possible way.

The gardener having a large garden to attend to, one which contains a selection of almost all the popular plants, hard and soft fruits, roses and shrubs, will need a wide range of pruning tools. True the outlay at the beginning may run to ten pounds or more, but well looked after and used with discretion the tools should last a lifetime. The small gardener with a number of young fruit trees to look after, some rose trees and a few shrubs which have not been allowed to get out of hand may be able to manage the whole of his pruning with a pair of medium size pruners and a pair of small size shears for the hedges.

CARE IN SELECTING TOOLS

When making a selection of pruning tools it is important to choose tools that "feel right". Like the properly balanced cricket bat which gives one confidence and is a pleasure to use and the spade which is moulded to one's touch and which makes light work of a heavy soil, so the pruning tools should feel equally balanced; they should handle right. Before making a final choice, examine a number of sizes, makes and styles and select the one most comfortable. But select a tool of reputable make, one which has been built up through the years as capable of performing the most efficient work; one which retains its sharp edges without becoming blunt, and without the spring which opens the blades becoming loose. Remember that when the pruning operations commence, several hundred cuts may have to be made and an efficient tool is an absolute necessity. An efficient tool will cost only a few shillings more than one which will prove of inferior quality, leave blisters on the hands and will bruise or tear the bark or new wood.

EFFICIENT SECATEURS

Excellent pruners for rose trees and for cutting new wood which should be cut clean and without any bruising are the new Pruneesy secateurs. The moving jaws will take any wood of reasonable size and will make a clean cut without squashing or bruising.

Ideal pruners for lady gardeners and for those who require a sharp, sturdy blade for pruning the hard wood of apples and pears is the Sword Pocket Pruner which opens and closes by a concealed spring. This pruner is capable of cutting the most stubborn wood with surgical precision; it is the ideal tool for top fruit trees of all ages.

For pruning shrubs of all sizes I would recommend the Rolcut secateurs which by their particular form are capable of making light work of the toughest shrubs and are light and easy to handle. I find that the old adage 'horses for courses' is equally applicable to pruners, each make should be used for its own particular job of pruning, though for the small gardener just one should be capable of performing all jobs efficiently. There are other efficient secateurs and I have only mentioned those I use in my own garden.

For reaching the top wood of taller trees, it is possible to obtain the same style pruners, but which are sold with wooden arms

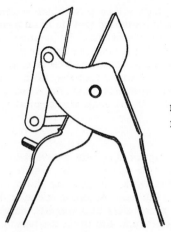

MOVING JAW-HEAD OF
PRUNEESY SECATEURS.

about 2 ft. in length. These are suitable for reaching top fruits
and older shrubs without the use of a ladder or steps and especially
are they useful for those plants with prickly leaves or stems, such
as many of the species of rose which are better pruned with the
hands and arms well out of the way of the strong thorns.

To reach to the top of older or neglected fruit and ornamental
trees, a long-arm is a most useful tool. This is a long piece of hard-
wood, about 7 ft. in length which is fitted with a cutting knife
worked by a lever which is held in the free hand. This cutting
tool is capable of removing the most stubborn branches up to
2 inches in diameter. Care should be taken that when using it,
the cutter blade is placed firmly against the wood before the lever
is used. Careless use will result in tearing of the wood.

USE OF THE SAW

To behead old trees and to remove stout top branches, a
ladder and a saw will be necessary, a saw also being essential
to remove stout lower branches of all types of tree and old,
neglected shrubs. For this, a cross-cut saw is best, but any
efficient and easily handled saw of reliable make will be suitable.
But as with secateurs, select a saw that you feel happy about and
do not obtain one too big. Both saws and pruners should be
cleaned and rubbed over with a fine oil after use. This is not so
much to prevent rusting for they will be mostly of rust-proof

steel, but oiling of the cutting part will keep the blade continually sharp. To keep the cutting part immersed in a tin of oil when not being used will prove even more efficient. The saw blade, too, should be kept as sharp as possible for cuts, no matter if they are made with secateurs or with a saw, must be as clean as possible. Bruising, crushing, tearing, and wood removed with a rough surface and edge will only cause trouble and rather than quickly heal over, will tend to die back. Sharp tools are essential to good pruning.

SHEARS AND THEIR USES

Shears for clipping hedges or conifers must also be kept sharp and oiled, for the same remarks apply. Shears which are not sharp and capable of efficient work will prolong the operation and leave the plants anything but neat. Again, in selecting shears, and they are obtainable in many sizes and weights, depending upon the amount of work to be done and upon the person using them. Here it may be said that one's tools should not be asked to perform tasks for which they are not made. For instance, to attempt to cut down a hedge containing a mass of thick, tough wood with a pair of light shears will ruin the tool without making a satisfactory job of the hedge. Where a saw is needed, use a saw and keep the shears and secateurs for the younger wood.

For most pruning jobs a pair of strong, pliable gloves is an essential, for not only will they act as a protection against injury from thorns when cutting back roses, but they will prevent any bruising of the hands where stout wood is being pruned during an operation possibly lasting several hours.

THE PRUNING KNIFE

An efficient pruning knife is also important and particularly is it essential for bark ringing, for notching, for removing suckers and young roots and for a host of other pruning jobs. The blade must be kept sharp by grinding, for a knife which is not sharp will cause more harm than good. With its particular shape, only a pruning knife must be used for the various operations. In addition to a pruning knife, to remove stout roots during the root pruning operation, a saw will be essential and this will also come in useful for removing stout top wood.

If cutting down a field hedge or a hedge that has become a mass of stout wood through age or neglect, a slashing hook, with either a short or long handle, will prove a handy tool if kept sharp.

They are exceedingly strong and if correctly used will be able to cut through wood up to 2 inches in diameter.

MAKING A CORRECT CUT

It is important to know just how to make a cut before the pruners are taken up. This should be made immediately above a vigorous outward bud and should be made with the slope of the cut away from the bud. The remaining wood above the cut will almost certainly die back to the bud and if more wood than necessary is allowed to remain, this may become a source of disease. The cut should be made clean, without bruising or tearing.

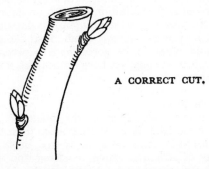

A CORRECT CUT.

It is also important to have handy a preparation for painting over the wounds caused by paring away diseased tissue and where branches have been severed. White lead paint is satisfactory and a new liquid fungicide called Medo will do the job even more efficiently.

One more thing remains to be said and that is, as soon as a tree or shrub has been pruned, the prunings must be cleared up and burnt. To leave them lying about the orchard or garden will only encourage disease which may eventually be transmitted to the healthy plants from which they were taken. It is preferable to make a small fire towards the end of each pruning day and to burn the rubbish whilst still fairly dry and before the shoots become trodden into the ground.

CHAPTER III

PRUNING ROSES

Hard v. Light Pruning — Study each Variety — When to
Prune — Moderate Pruning — Planting and Pruning new
Trees — Standard Roses — Suckers — Pruning for Succes-
sional flowering — Weeping Standards — Correct way to
Prune — Roses indoors.

BECAUSE there are few gardens in England where a rose tree does
not grow, perhaps it would be appropriate to begin this book
with the pruning of roses over which controversy has continued
through the years. Whether to prune hard or lightly has still to be
definitely decided and whereas one gardener suggests pruning
hard to obtain blooms of exhibition quality, an equally know-
ledgeable rose enthusiast is most definite in his contention that a
rose bush should be pruned scarcely at all. That the most satisfactory way would seem to be somewhere between the two
theories seems to please no one, yet I am certain that it is the most
successful method.

HARD V. LIGHT PRUNING

Severe pruning not only deprives the plant of wood and
foliage which is so valuable in converting foods from the atmo-
sphere so necessary in building up a sturdy tree, but also ensures
that the quantity of bloom is much restricted and we cannot
expect to enjoy any worthwhile display until early autumn.
Against this argument, the bloom will be of exhibition quality
and though the greatest amount will be produced in autumn,
perhaps this is all to the good. But if pruning is moderate, top
quality blooms will still be enjoyed and the bushes will continue
to bear their blooms over a longer period. The bush is also capable
of utilising its foliage to build up a plant of healthy new wood
and a vigorous root system.

Too light pruning will not only give a vigorous display in
early summer and very little bloom in autumn, but the blooms
will be of inferior quality even for the house and the tree will
eventually lose its vigour with having to carry too much super-
fluous wood. But much depends upon climate and variety, and
these factors must receive consideration before any pruning at
all is done.

I have found that roses growing in the South, West Midlands
and South West, should be pruned harder than elsewhere in

Britain, for they make more early summer growth and if not pruned fairly hard will bear a mass of small blooms until mid-August and will by then have 'shot their bolt'. They will not possess the vigour which is characteristic of the modern hybrid teas, to come again in autumn. Elsewhere moderate pruning should be done, for the plants will come along only slowly during early summer and will continue to bear a quantity of top quality blooms from July until Christmas.

STUDY EACH VARIETY

As far as variety is concerned in Hybrid Tea Roses, some are exceedingly vigorous, and which if not cut back moderately hard will bear their blooms on stems as much as 4 ft. tall. The white varieties possess exceptional vigour, especially the old Hybrid Perpetual, Frau Karl Druschki, which if not pruned fairly hard will reach a height of more than 5 ft. by autumn and spoil any bedding display by its vigour. The creamy-white, Mandarin, and the pure, White Swan, are also tall growing.

But there are also weak growing varieties which make only thin, twiggy wood and which require no other pruning than the removal of dead wood and cutting back the tips of the shoots. Included in this section are the lovely bi-colours, Lamplighter and Sultane, and the deep crimson favourite Etoile de Hollande are all of slender growth.

The polyantha and floribunda roses also require but little pruning other than the removal of dead and unwanted wood, a little thinning out of the bush at the centre and pruning the tips of strong growing shoots. They may be said to require only 'light pruning'.

WHEN TO PRUNE

When to prune is again a matter of climate. Whether pruning moderately or hard, the shoot must be cut back to a vigorous bud pointing to an outward position. If the bud is caught by frost and damaged, there may be no other suitable bud on that shoot to take its place. So no pruning should be done until all fear of frost damage has passed. As roses are extremely hardy, frost damage may be taken to mean severe frost and this is not likely to be experienced later than mid-April in the most exposed gardens of the North. In the South and West Midlands, pruning may be done at the end of March; whilst farther south, early March pruning will be in order. But do not be in too big a hurry to use the pruners, roses are slow to come into new growth and it is better to be sure rather than sorry.

My own method is to cut out all dead wood at Christmas when the plants have finished flowering and will by then have lost their leaves. At the same time any very long shoots are shortened back one-third. This is to prevent the winter winds causing too much movement of the plant, thereby loosening the roots. Also, any suckers are cut away and the plants made firm around the stem. They will then be well able to withstand the severest of weather. Then, depending upon district and prevailing weather, cold winds being able to cause as much damage to the new buds as will frost, pruning proper is carried out between early March and the end of April. Then is the time to cut away any shoots that are interfering with each other and where excess growth is tending to upset the balance of the bush this should be cut back to allow the other part of the plant to develop. Then cut back any weak shoots and here the characteristics of the particular variety will provide the answer as to whether the shoot is weak by nature or by constitution.

MODERATE PRUNING

Finally, and this is where controversy arises, cut back last year's wood or stems to stimulate the plant or for one of the reasons as previously described. To prune hard means to cut back all wood to within 3 or 4 inches of ground level, cutting back to a single eye pointing outwards. To prune moderately means to cut back to a bud at about half the length of the average growth made by the stems the previous season. Light pruning means to cut back only to the first or second eye from the top of the stems.

If the blooms have been cut in large numbers for home decoration during summer and autumn, only light pruning may be required. The opinion of rose specialists now seems to be against severe pruning except when new bushes have just been planted, but my own experience, and I grow thousands of roses, is that moderate pruning, depending upon variety, will give the best all round results.

If only light pruning is being done, this may be carried out over Christmas at the same time as excess growth is being pruned for the winter and when the bushes are being cleared of dead wood.

In pruning old and neglected bushes which are often blooming on thick stems 5 ft. tall, the same care must be taken as when

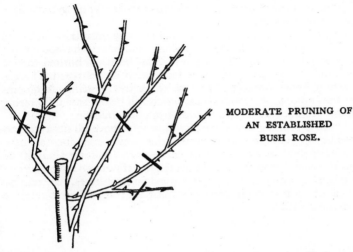

MODERATE PRUNING OF
AN ESTABLISHED
BUSH ROSE.

renovating neglected fruit trees and that is to prune a little at a time, cutting back new wood to a half of last season's growth and cutting away any dead and 'woody' stems.

PLANTING NEW TREES

When planting new rose trees, and November and December are the ideal months so that the roots have time to settle in before frost and snow, do no pruning at planting time but in spring cut back the shoots to two buds from the base; April 1st being the most suitable time. This hard pruning will induce the plant to build up a sturdy foundation and henceforth only moderate pruning will be necessary. It will generally be found that much of the wood of roses that has been moved will tend to die back almost to the base and so hard pruning is always to be recommended in this case.

STANDARD ROSES

The same hard pruning will be necessary for the standard form, for with all roses it must be remembered that when moved, the roots take with them few fibres and little soil and so should not be asked to provide nourishment for a large amount of foliage until the new rooting system has become established. If the wood is not cut hard back the plant may never completely recover from having to support excess foliage whilst still struggling to build up a strong root system.

Again it is required with both bush and standard forms, to build up a sturdy framework with vigorous new wood at the bottom of the tree. When once this has been established then it will only be necessary to prune moderately as described. There is nothing more unsightly than to see a tree bearing its blooms at the end of long, woody stems which will be the case if flowering stems are not encouraged to form from base buds.

Future pruning of standards will be to remove all decayed and weakly growth and to remove stems which may be too near together. New wood should be cut back to about one-half of the new season's growth, but the same remarks apply in the case of the less vigorous varieties as explained for bush trees. Any unduly long, unripened shoots should be cut back still further to retain a balanced head.

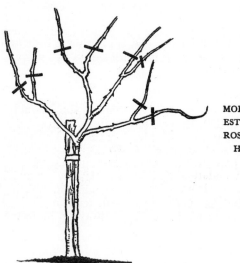

MODERATE PRUNING OF
ESTABLISHED STANDARD
ROSE, ALL DEAD WOOD
HAVING ALSO BEEN
REMOVED.

SUCKERS

The question of suckers continually forming on bush trees and climbers is always one demanding attention. The trouble of distinguishing between genuine new shoots and a sucker is often difficult, but if the soil is carefully scraped away from the base, it will be noticed that a genuine shoot is formed above the union of scion and rootstock even though this may be covered over with soil. A sucker arises from a root and it is little use severing this at ground level, for it would only grow again. Remove the soil around the sucker to disclose the point of contact with the root, then sever it at the point of contact by using a sharp knife. Then replace the soil and tread firmly for it is generally on insecure trees that suckers form and will use up much of the nourishment required by the tree if not removed.

PRUNING FOR SUCCESSION

Those who possess a large garden might find it advantageous to prune for a succession of bloom. Some trees, even of the same variety, may be pruned harder than others, whilst some may be only very lightly pruned. This would ensure that there would be a continuous supply of bloom from the end of June until the year end; a six months continuous supply. Hard pruning need not be too severe and light pruning should be sufficient to retain the shape of the tree and keep it vigorous and free of all unwanted wood.

WEEPING STANDARDS

Now rightly so popular, the weeping roses require very different pruning treatment than ordinary standards. It will be noticed that they will make very much more wood which will be of a thin, twiggy nature. It will be necessary to reduce this each year, cutting out almost all the old or previous season's wood and removing much of the new season's wood where it appears crowded. Those shoots which are almost reaching to the ground should be cut back to retain the correct shape of the head. All pruning should be done early in autumn when the tree will have finished flowering. This will make room for vigorous new spring growth.

CORRECT WAY TO PRUNE

Although many millions of bush roses are pruned each year little care is ever taken to ensure a correct cut. This should slope away from an outer bud and should be made about half an inch above the bud. Too close cutting may harm the bud and cutting too far away will leave a piece of wood which will soon decay and which may also cause the new shoot to decay also.

CORRECT CUT (A) AN
OUTWARD BUD.

CLIMBING ROSES
Correct pruning methods are described in Chapter 4.

ROSES INDOORS
A climbing rose makes a most attractive plant for covering the walls of a lean-to greenhouse. Grown well and pruned with care they will remain healthy for at least a quarter of a century and will bloom almost continuously from early April (depending upon the amount of spring sunshine) until the darker days of November. After planting in a prepared bed, cut back the main stems to about 9 inches of the base to a strong outwards bud, then for the next three years, until the plant has covered the wall; only weak growth should be removed. Afterwards give the same pruning as for open air climbers (Chapter IV.).

Bush roses in pots or beds and grown indoors should be constantly pruned back to three or four healthy base buds and this pruning is generally done with the cutting of the blooms. To obtain roses for Christmas, all shoots should be cut back to three buds on October 1st and the plants given a heavy mulching with decayed manure. Control of watering and of temperature will bring on the blooms as required.

CHAPTER IV

CLIMBING AND WALL PLANTS

Climbers requiring different pruning technique — Ceanothus
— Clematis — Coronilla glauca — Cydonia Japonica —
Elaeagnus — Garrya elliptica — Honeysuckle — Hydrangea
petiolaris — Ivy — Jasmine — Magnolia — Myrtle —
Pyracantha — Roses — Vines — Wisteria.

CLIMBING plants may be divided into a number of groups each requiring different pruning treatment. First there are the self-clinging plants, the ivies, virginian creeper and Hydrangea petiolaris which require occasional clipping back with shears to allow the more colourful new foliage to break through. Then there are the real climbing wall plants, the climbing roses, the honey-suckles and clematis in all their various forms, which require considerable detail to be given to their pruning. Again, there are the wall shrubs, the ceanothus and buddleias which may be grown in the open as shrubs or equally well against a wall, and these require the constant cutting out of dead wood and cutting back the flower heads when the blooms have finished. There is also yet another group, those plants which require the spurring back of laterals to form blossom buds, and here I am thinking of the wisteria, which is given much the same treatment as espalier pears, which may also be used to add colour to a wall.

CEANOTHUS. Not quite hardy in the most exposed gardens, this superb summer-flowering plant which produces its powder-blue flowers on the shoots formed during spring and early summer of the same season, should be very lightly thinned during March to encourage the formation of new growth during the next weeks. The species *C. dentatus*, the hardiest, tends to form rather more twiggy wood which should be kept thinned out.

CLEMATIS. Next to the rose in popularity as a climbing plant is the clematis and its species. It is not generally realised that the garden clematis we know so well is divided into four groups.

(a) The Jackmanni and viticella groups, for which pruning is the same, for both are extremely hardy and as they bloom late in the year, bearing their flowers on the young shoots formed during the early spring, new wood should be cut back to within several inches of the old wood and the time to do this is early in March. The variety, Perle d' Azur also blooms on the old wood and so should be left almost entirely unpruned except to remove any dead wood. Of the viticella group the petunia-red Ernest Markham, and the rose coloured Margot Koster are outstanding varieties.

(b)   The lanuginosa section bears its flowers on both the old and the new wood and over a long period, from June till early September. It is therefore advisable to thin out any weak or decayed growth and this should be done early in the New Year so as not to interfere with early buds. The double sky-blue Prince Henry and the pink, King George V are attractive members of this section.

(c)   The patens group which includes the multi-coloured Nellie Moser, blooms only on the old wood and comes and goes during the month of June. It is therefore advisable to do no pruning until the plant makes so much growth that it needs some of the older wood thinning out.

It is important to cut back to a good bud about 12 inches from the base all newly planted clematis which operation should be done in March or April and after that it should be remembered that more plants are spoilt by too much pruning than by any other cause.

CORONILLA *glauca*. This is a delightful wall plant for a seaside garden with its grey-green foliage and vetch-like flowers providing colour the whole year round. The long, graceful shoots should be cut back to retain the shape and this and any removal of dead wood should be done after the summer flush of blossom and vigorous new growth has ended, mid-autumn being the most suitable time.

CYDONIA *japonica*. The Japanese Quince, with its richly coloured blooms, like wild roses, produced in abundance in early spring, is one of the most striking of our hardy wall plants. The plants should be trained rather than pruned much, for they tend to produce shoots in an outward direction away from the wall and these should be removed in November together with any decayed or surplus wood.

ELAEAGNUS. With its vivid olive green and golden foliage, this is a superb plant for a cold wall. It is evergreen and pruning should consist of cutting out the old wood in May each year.

Photo: *Rolcut*

1. Range of efficient tree pruners and secateurs for fruit trees, roses and shrubs.

2. Apple, LANE'S PRINCE ALBERT which has been carefully pruned to counteract its dropping habit.

Photo: *J. E. Downward*

3. A well tended orchard.

Photo: R. A. Malby & Co.

4. Cordon fruit trees, well train
and correctly spurred. Note
fan-trained trees in bac
ground.

Photo: R. A. Malby & Co.

GARRYA *elliptica*. A charming evergreen for a northerly wall where it bears masses of green catkins from early March until May. It should be given much the same treatment as the Wisteria, cutting back the laterals during summer to form spurs from which the catkins are borne.

HONEYSUCKLE. The climbing loniceras, to give the fragrant honeysuckles their correct name, require almost no pruning. Here again they may be divided into two groups, the early flowering *L. japonica* section, more vigorous growers than the Dutch Honeysuckles and which bear their flowers on the wood or shoots formed the previous summer. Pruning will consist of thinning out some of the old wood early in summer and the pinching back of some of the new shoots.

The second group comprises the Dutch honeysuckles, early and later flowering, and this is the plant we are more familiar with. Bearing their blooms on both the old and new wood and not being as vigorous as the japonica group, the only pruning necessary is to cut out any unwanted or dead wood in late autumn.

HYDRANGEA *petiolaris*. This is a rapid clinging climber with ivy-like foliage and white flowers in no way resembling the garden hydrangea. It may be necessary to cut back after flowering for it makes considerable growth. It should be kept in bounds rather than be given any severe pruning.

IVY. Botanically called Hedera, the variegated ivies are valuable plants for rapidly covering a northerly wall. The shoots should be prevented growing too closely round window frames and near roof tiles as they will push their way underneath and dislodge them. So clip back the young shoots away from window and roof and every other year put the shears over the whole plant clipping it well back to encourage new foliage and to keep the ivy free from dead wood and leaves of trees which collect in neglected ivy.

JASMINE. This is a climber we all love in both the winter and summer flowering forms. *J. nudiflorum*, the yellow winter jasmine which remains in bloom from early December until March, should be lightly cut back as soon as it has finished blooming,

B

merely shortening the new wood and removing any decayed growth. Excessive pruning will spoil the display.

The summer flowering *J. officinale major* which bears trusses of fragrant white flowers requires much the same pruning when flowering has finished in early autumn. It tends to make a little more woody growth which should be thinned accordingly. The evergreen June flowering *J. Reevesi* should be thinned out after blooming to allow new growth to form during summer to carry next season's flowers.

MAGNOLIA. Delightful either as a wall plant or as a bush where given the protection of a wall it will bear its spectacular water-lily-like blossoms on leafless stems early in spring. The creamy-white, *M. Soulangiana*, which blooms abundantly even when quite small, and the plum coloured *M. Lennei* should be pruned only when absolutely necessary, as the cuts, like those of the cherry, take considerable time to heal over. Any cutting must be done in June after flowering.

The evergreen species *M. grandiflora*, which bears its creamy, lemon-scented blooms during summer, will stand any amount of pruning (if necessary) and this should consist of the removal of unwanted wood in early autumn.

MYRTLE. *Myrtus communis*, an evergreen with its sprays of sweetly scented white flowers from late July until September is a charming wall plant, but should be pruned only in late April for fear of frost damage. Pruning consists of cutting back the old wood and retaining the shape of the tree.

PYRACANTHA. The firethorn is a wall plant that delights us with its vivid berries during winter. Its habit is neat and close-jointed and the flowers being formed on the last season's wood should not be cut back. The only necessary pruning is to thin out some of the old twiggy wood in spring and to remove any shoots which tend to spoil the shape.

ROSES. There are two distinct types of climbing roses, both of which require different pruning techniques. They are:—

(*a*) The Climbing Hybrid Tea Roses which are climbing forms of many of the lovely Tea Roses we know so well, Peace and Crimson Glory and Ena Harkness, and

(b)   The Wichuraiana Climbers and Ramblers which are also
used in the weeping form for standards, such varieties
as Excelsa and Dorothy Perkins. Of recent years the
Climbing Hybrid Teas have risen to great heights of
popularity, so let us first consider the requirements of
this class.

These roses bear their next season's crop chiefly on the older
wood and so require little pruning apart from removing any dead
wood and some thinning out of laterals which by the more
vigorous growers like Peace and Emily Gray are often formed in
too large numbers.

Again with this class, when planting a new tree, do not cut back
too vigorously or there will be the chance of it reverting to the
bush type again. The wood should be cut back to about 15 inches
of the base and to suitable outward buds. The remaining stems
and the new shoots which will grow from the buds will be the
framework of the tree. Any thinning out of lateral growth and
the removal of any too numerous new shoots should be done
during early winter.

The necessity of removing any suckers is also important, but
take care not to cut out the vigorous young shoots which may
arise from the base and which may be trained to form flowering
wood for the lower part of the tree which may eventually become
bare.

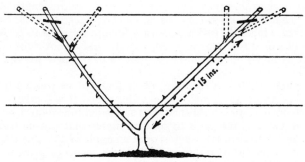

A NEWLY PLANTED CLIMBING TEA ROSE CUT BACK TO SUITABLE BUDS.

With the Wichuraiana Climbers and Ramblers, these form
their blooms on the new wood formed during the previous summer
and so all old and useless wood except of course the wood which
composes the framework of the tree, should be removed in
autumn when the plant has finished flowering.

The newly planted tree may be cut back more vigorously than
in the case of Climbing Tea Roses, to about 6 inches of the
base and to suitable buds. Later, any weak growth should be
pinched back and the more vigorous stems be allowed to grow
unchecked except if they should become too vigorous. The aim
should be to cover the wall with bloom from the bottom upwards
and should the main stems make too much growth they should
be cut back to persuade lateral buds to 'break'.

It will be found that certain varieties such as the charming
single yellow Mermaid will need almost no pruning after the
newly planted tree has been cut back to vigorous buds. Some
varieties are vigorous by nature, others make little growth other
than they will require. But as we said in Chapter 1, study each
variety before any pruning is done, then prune entirely on its
merits.

VINES. The ornamental vines or vitis, is a most valuable quick
growing plant for covering an unsightly wall or trellis. They
possess an added value in that their leaves take on the most
glorious autumn tints which are retained well into the winter.
None is more brilliant than *V. Coignetiae*, with its attractive
heart-shaped leaves, and it is a most vigorous grower. Its main
stem will quickly reach the top of a trellis and they should then
be cut back so that they will form laterals down the length of the
stem. Then each lateral should be pinched back in December to
two eyes: especially is this necessary for the vigorous *V. purpurea*.
After two or three years any old wood should be cut right out to
admit as much air and light as possible to the new wood.

WISTERIA. This is a climbing plant that can be trained in the
spur formation very much like espalier pears. It will take a year
or two to become established and a young tree should be cut
back to two healthy buds to provide shoots that can be trained
either in the horizontal position or at an angle of 45°. The laterals
formed along the main stems will make vigorous growth and
these should be spurred back to but five leaves during mid-
summer to make blossom-bearing spurs. These may again be cut

back to two buds during winter. If not cut back in this way the
laterals will make too much leaf and the plant will be clothed in
foliage rather than in blossom.

CHAPTER V

FLOWERING SHRUBS

The need for Pruning Shrubs — Acer — Arbutus — Azalea
— Berberis — Buddleia — Chimonanthus fragrans — Cornus
— Cotoneaster — Cytisus — Daphne — Deutzia — Escallonia
— Forsythia — Fuchsia — Hamamelis — Hibiscus —
Hydrangea — Kerria — Lavender — Lilac — Osmarea —
Philadelphus — Rhododendron — Ribes — Rose — Rosemary
—Santolina — Senecio — Syringa — Veronica — Viburnum
—Weigela.

For the first years of their life, flowering shrubs remain colourful
and neat in their habit; we plant them in quantity because most
of them are inexpensive and when once in the ground it is
imagined that they can be forgotten. This, however, is quite the
wrong attitude to take. Without gentle pruning from the beginning the shrubs build up far too much old wood which if pruned
vigorously in the hope that the shrub can be given a new life,
tends to die back instead of producing vigorous new shoots and
we are left with an ugly looking plant comprised of little else but
thick woody shoots almost devoid of life. A little gentle pruning
from the beginning will work wonders, the plant will remain
vigorous and a mass of bloom and new wood over a very long
period. What is more there will be no crowding out of a perhaps
equally beautiful but less vigorous variety by one which will
make excessive growth if not kept under control. We see this
often in a shrubbery which was well and carefully planted in the
first instance only to become a jumbled mass of coarse growth in
the years ahead with the less vigorous shrubs prevented from
flowering and being smothered by those which will grow rampant
if allowed to do so.

Then many gardeners who do prune and keep their shrubbery
tidy and healthy, neglect to make a study of the individual shrubs
with the result that some are pruned in autumn when they should
receive attention in spring with the disappointment that they do

not bloom when they should, and maybe not at all. Every variety must be studied and pruned on its merits and it is surprising how diverse are their requirements. By giving regular pruning it is possible to plant closer, the shrubs then smothering weeds and giving a bank of colour in a very short time. Be sure to plant the low shrubs to the front of the border with the taller ones behind for no amount of pruning can change their natural habit. Then there are those suitable for a cold, northerly position and those that must be given a sunny border in which to ripen their wood.

ACER. There are a number of bush Maples whose foliage takes on the richest colourings in autumn. *A. Ginnola* and *A. griseum* both have a vigorous habit, but apart from removing old wood they require no pruning.

ARBUTUS. Evergreen and known as the strawberry tree which does well on limestone soils, and also near the sea. Of slow growth, but the old wood should be kept to a minimum by cutting back in April to allow new wood to develop.

AZALEA. Both the evergreen and deciduous species being so slow growing, little pruning is necessary other than cutting out dead wood which continually forms.

BERBERIS. Many of the evergreen berberis make such strong, woody growth that this should be constantly cut away to allow to make room for new wood which will carry the fresh green foliage.

BUDDLEIA. The new hybrids such as Charming, pale pink, and the deep purple, Royal Red, are now so much admired that this plant has become one of our most popular shrubs. The long sprays in July are borne on the wood formed during early summer, so to retain the vigour of the plant it may be cut back to 12 inches of the base as soon as flowering has ended. In this way the shrub is kept compact and vigorous. However, where there is space, the buddleia will make a magnificent specimen if allowed to retain much of its old wood when it will attain a height of 12-15 ft. Dead and unwanted wood should be removed in early autumn.

Buddleia globosa, which bears its tiny orange-like blooms on the previous year's wood in early summer has quite a different habit and should not be pruned; only dead, twiggy wood being removed in the autumn.

CHIMONANTHUS *fragrans*. The slow growing sweetly-scented wintersweet bears its bloom on the previous season's wood and except for the cutting out of dead wood and slightly reducing the main stems to encourage new wood to form, no other pruning is required.

CORNUS. The Dogwoods comprise a large number of species and provide colour with their blossoms, fruit and foliage throughout the year. *C. alba Westonbirt* is strong growing and must have old and excess wood cut out each spring. *C. Mas* which bears fluffy, yellow flowers in March, requires some thinning in late autumn.

COTONEASTER. This is the name which embraces a wide variety of small glossy-leaved plants which cover themselves in a mass of scarlet berries in autumn and winter formed from blossom which appears in spring. Most of them are slow growing and produce their new wood from the old and so require little pruning except to thin out some of the old wood when growth becomes too thick. *C. Simonsi* of tall, upright growth may be shortened back if it has covered the low wall intended or if it is growing away too strongly.

CYTISUS. The hybrid brooms, now so popular for a shrubbery, require very careful handling from the beginning. A little careful pruning of the main stems to encourage them to 'break' to form new flowering shoots should be done but if allowed to grow away until they form much old wood this cannot be cut back in later years as it will most probably die back altogether. Old brooms which have become tall and woody are the most difficult of all trees to renovate.

DAPHNE. All the daphnes are but slow growing from the March flowering Mezereum to the June flowering *D. Collina* and except for the cutting back of a shoot which may have made more growth than others so as to build up a shapely bush, no other pruning is necessary.

DEUTZIA. Producing their flowers on the young wood, the deutzias are naturally neat of habit, but flowering will be more profuse if the older wood is cut out in early autumn after flowering.

ESCALLONIA. See Chapter XIII.

FORSYTHIA. Producing its masses of rich golden bells in early spring, both the erect growing *F. spectabilis* and the arching *F. suspensa* should be pruned back in late spring after flowering, removing old wood and any sprigs that have made excessive growth and are taking away some of the beauty of shape.

FUCHSIA. The hardy varieties should be cut back to a few inches of the base early in spring (the dead wood will provide winter protection) as it is on the new season's growth that the blooms will form in late summer.

HAMAMELIS. The Witch Hazels, which bear their claw-like flowers on leafless stems in early spring, require no pruning other than the cutting of a sprig showing buds in late February to open indoors.

HIBISCUS. The plants must be given full sun to ripen their wood, the flowers being carried at the top of the new growth formed during spring and early summer. So reduce the pre-season's wood in March and remove altogether any worthless or overcrowded wood.

HYDRANGEA. Pruning for shape and for quality of bloom is important. A young plant should not be allowed to carry more than 3-4 flower heads and this number may be increased to a dozen as the plant matures. Old wood should be cut out or if a young plant does not carry excess wood, only the faded flower heads may be removed after flowering, cutting back to two buds of the new wood.

The species *H. macrophylla* with its feathery pinky-white blooms will require only the faded flowers removing in autumn and any worthless old wood cutting out.

KERRIA *japonica* or Jew's Mallow and a particular favourite of mine. It bears masses of double orange blooms in early summer and after flowering any old wood should be removed and where new shoots have made excess growth these should be cut back in early July.

LAVENDER. So many lavender hedges are spoilt by allowing growth to become straggling that some form of pruning should be done, but this should be done almost from the beginning. Like the broom, the lavender quickly becomes a mass of lanky coarse wood if not kept trimmed each spring so that new wood is continually being established. When once a lavender has formed a mass of old wood, to revive it may mean to kill it or it will take several years to make fresh growth and bloom abundantly again.

LILAC. This must surely be the most popular of all flowering shrubs, but prune but little for they resent any severe cutting back. Remove any old and unwanted wood in July and at the same time cut back the dead flower stems to a lateral newly forming. It is on this that next year's flowers will form.

Lilacs are often troubled with suckers. The area around the base where the suckers form should be scraped free of soil and the suckers severed with a sharp knife. The soil should be made very firm when returned.

OSMAREA *Burkwoodii*. This is a most handsome shrub with neat foliage and which covers itself with a mass of white sweetly-perfumed flowers in May. It is superb as a hedge and the only pruning required is to cut out some of the old wood and trim back the most vigorous shoots in mid-summer.

PHILADELPHUS. The mock orange is almost as popular as the lilac and is of much more vigorous habit. It is on the newly formed shoots that next year's flowers will form so cut back the dead flowering shoots to a new lateral as soon as late summer flowering has ended and at the same time cut away all surplus and dead wood which the plant makes in quantity. This is one of the shrubs that requires regular and quite hard pruning.

RHODODENDRON. Both the dwarf and large-flowered hybrids require little pruning except to remove the dead flower heads so that the new wood can form buds for next season. Cut back to a strong wood bud or lateral and at the same time remove all unproductive wood.

RIBES. The Flowering Currant has long been an old favourite and being a strong grower should be kept in shape by thinning out much of the twiggy wood in early summer after flowering.

ROSE. Although there is a large number of species, almost all require little in the way of pruning apart from removing old, decayed wood. The Austrian briars bloom on the old wood, similarly the Banksian Roses, and so little should be removed except to retain the vigour of the tree.

The Penzance Briars, being excessively vigorous, will require rather more thinning and especially should the long new shoots be cut back in early March to encourage the shoots to furnish the lower portions with new growth.

The lovely Provence Roses come into bloom early and should be pruned in February. Old wood must be cut away and young vigorous shoots must be cut back to a robust bud otherwise the habit of the plant will tend to become weak.

The Japanese or Rogosa roses which bear large orange fruits in late autumn following summer flowering, make dense growth and must be cut back to 10 inches of the base each January or be very severely thinned otherwise the plant will be a mass of growth which will bear little new wood.

Moss roses should be pruned in February, much of the old wood being cut away and the new shoots being shortened to about half the previous season's wood.

ROSEMARY. *R. officinalis* with its blue flowers, and *R. alba* the uncommon white form, need to be kept tidy by having much of the older wood cut away each autumn and as with the lavender this should not be left untouched until the plant becomes a mass of thick wood producing few new shoots. Gentle pruning should be done from the beginning.

SANTOLINA. The Cotton Lavender with its attractive silver-grey foliage is a valuable low shrub for an exposed garden. The plant should be kept in shape by cutting back some of last season's growth in March. Much of the old wood may be removed in autumn after flowering.

SENECIO *Grayi*. Most of us know this silvery-leaved shrub with its masses of attractive yellow daisy-like flowers, so often found at the seaside. It will become untidy if not regularly pruned, cutting some of the old wood out in autumn and at the same time trimming back the vigorous new shoots.

SYRINGA. Species of the lilac possess extreme beauty and most have a drooping habit with slender arching branches, rather like the buddleia. The only pruning necessary is to cut back the flower branches late in summer and at the time to thin out old shoots.

VERONICA. Of compact habit, the veronicas always grow well near the sea, covering themselves in a mass of bloom from July until November. In March, established plants should be cut back to keep them bushy, much of the old wood being cut back to persuade it to 'break' into new growth. Like similar shrubs, the veronicas will tend to make an excess of thick, woody stems if not kept continually pruned.

VIBURNUM. Here is a group of plants having a wide variety of forms and requiring different treatment as to pruning. *V. fragrans*, which flowers through winter, needs only dead wood cutting out in spring. *V. carlcephalum*, flowering early in summer, may require old wood cutting out in July; whilst *V. opulus sterile*, the familiar old 'snowball tree,' should have the flower stems shortened back in autumn and any excess growth removed. *V. tinus*, an evergreen which makes a valuable screen should be cut back if it makes too vigorous growth.

WEIGELA. This is a summer flowering shrub which requires constant pruning to retain its free flowering habit and shape. This is a plant which if left untended will rapidly become a mass of dead wood and there will be few flowers. Prune early in autumn cutting out the old wood vigorously.

CHAPTER VI

PRUNING ORNAMENTAL TREES

Renovating neglected trees — Pruning specimen trees — Conifers — Individual treatment of ornamental trees — Acer —Almond — Ash — Beech — Birch — Cerasus — Chestnut —Crataegus — Davidia — Elm — Hornbeam — Laburnum — Mulberry — Oak — Poplar — Prunus — Pyrus — Sorbus — Walnut — Willow.

THOUGH fancy and ornamental trees and evergreens are being planted in continually larger numbers on account of their ease of cultivation, so many become of untidy appearance through their being given no attention at all. Not only is their shape seriously harmed, but the tree may have become a mass of decayed wood. Again, broken branches which have been long neglected, may have left scars and tears on the bark which is not only unsightly, but will be a constant source of infection.

RENOVATING NEGLECTED TREES

First then, the neglected tree. Anyone who has taken over an old garden will find trees with large numbers of their lower branches quite dead and which will snap off at pressure, whilst there will be numbers of branches which will have made such vigorous growth that not only will they be better removed so as to admit more light and air to the tree, but which may be extending right into the foliage of other trees and shrubs causing distortion and overcrowding. But first look over each tree to remove dead lower wood which is playing no part in the life of the tree or the beauty of the garden. These branches should be cut away with a saw flush up to the stem or trunk from which they are being removed. At the same time all broken pieces still remaining on the trunk must be cut out for these will be no more than a source of infection. The Scots Pine and Silver Birch are trees that always carry much dead wood if neglected. Removal of this wood will allow more room and sunlight to reach those plants growing beneath them even if they be only berberis.

Then look to see if the tree is carrying any low branches which are surplus to the shape and beauty of the tree. Larch, beech and laburnum may frequently be seen with such branches which are better cut away. Cut right to the bark for then the cut will quickly form a callus which will cover the wound and so prevent rot setting in and in the case of the *Prunus* and *Cerasus* families, the ornamental plums and cherries, this will keep the risk of introducing silver leaf disease to a minimum. An additional precaution will be to paint the wound with white lead paint to keep out wet and disease until the callus has formed.

Frequently, trees are found which have had branches torn away sometime in the past. These have formed dead stumps which have later come away from the main trunk leaving a large, ugly gap. This should be cleaned round with a sharp knife, be painted with white lead paint and should then be filled in with cement as described in the chapter on Renovating Old Fruit Trees. It should be said that all work on pruning and renovating should be done between November and March; conifers during November and December, whilst the sap is at its lowest; and the ornamental and eating plums and cherries should be pruned only in late spring so that gumming is reduced to a minimum. This is most troublesome during wet, cold weather when the wound will not heal.

Mis-shapen trees should be beautified as much as possible by having badly formed branches removed. This will encourage the formation of younger shoots which will help to re-shape the tree though it should be said that a young tree, carefully looked after will build up a frame that will provide beauty of shape for a life-time without any undue attention and cutting and obviously the less a tree is pruned the better.

As most trees are to be found growing in groups, they should be surveyed as a whole, rather than individually, for a specimen tree standing on its own may require quite different pruning and thinning than if growing with others. Position, too, will have much to do with any pruning. It may be necessary to form a wind-break when as much branch growth as possible should be allowed to remain, except of course, where decayed.

PRUNING SPECIMEN TREES

The specimen tree, the weeping types, and those which it is necessary to train to a desired shape, such as a tree which may be viewed from the house or which will form the focus point in the garden must be carefully trained from the beginning. Those of weeping habit may be trained, by taking the leading shoots right round the tree and cutting away much of the unwanted lateral and centre growth, to form a tent of rich foliage. Here it is necessary to keep the centre of the tree around the main trunk or stem free of weak and excessive growth, the accent must be placed on the outer pendulous branches. Should any branch tend to be making more growth than the others, it should be fastened to a tall stake for eighteen months and bent to an upwards direction to check the flow of sap.

The ornamental or flowering tree selected for making a specimen with evenly spaced branches must be given careful pruning right from the start. First it will be necessary to select branches forming in opposite directions and this will be the framework of the tree. Other wood should be cut away, except of course the leader shoot, and as the main stem attains height other suitable branches are selected until the well-shaped tree has been formed, taking possibly twenty years or more. All shoots and suckers

appearing at the bottom of the stem should be regularly cut away.
Indeed on no trees should suckers be allowed to remain.

Those trees required as specimens for small gardens may need
to have their too vigorous growth restricted. This is done by
removing the leader shoot when the desired height has been
reached or side branches may be 'stopped'. With cherries which
tend to 'gum', root pruning should be done, possibly in alternate
years, removing the roots from one side of the tree during one
year, the opposite roots at another occasion. This will limit the
amount of new wood, but at the same time will not prove too big
a check on the functions of the roots which would upset the
balance of the tree.

Building up the tree by degrees will in later years not necessi-
tate the dreadful butchering of the trees seen so often along the
roads of our cities and in public parks where the trees have been
so cut as to have been deprived of all natural form and beauty.

CONIFERS

Correctly planted the true conifers should need little pruning.
Yew and Golden Retinospora may be clipped frequently to make
a splendid hedge, but specimen trees will require little attention.
It is important to study the ultimate shape of all conifers so that
any unwanted side shoots may be cut away in early winter, for a
branching habit is not required unless it be certain of the dwarf
species used for a rockery or trough garden. Here continual
cutting back will produce that old, gnarled effect, so often seen
with the conifers growing in their natural surroundings, often
between large rocks where they have rooted in a few inches of
soil. The dwarfing of young conifers is done by pinching back
much of the fresh green foliage in mid-summer.

It may also happen that conifers with a horizontal branch habit
may form one or more branches of considerably longer length
than others. It will be necessary to remove the leader shoot of
these long branches so as to prevent further growth. This will
allow the shorter branches to attain the same size before being
'stopped'. Thus the tree will ultimately be of perfect proportions.
Horizontal branches which may be formed too close together
should be cut away in November, the wound being painted with
tar to keep out disease.

Those conifers with an upright habit are frequently caught
by cold winds, the foliage turning brown and gradually dying
back. This should be carefully removed with the pruners to allow

fresh, green foliage to take its place. Often the same trouble is found if the trees are growing too close together, but here little can be done except to thin out overcrowded foliage.

Acer. The Maples, of which family the Sycamore is a member, are reasonably fast growing and will need those excessively vigorous branches shortening over winter.

Almond. Where they can be given a dry climate and plenty of lime in the soil, the flowering almonds are quick growing. To build up a balanced tree the shoots should be pinched back in summer to encourage the formation of side growth. Dead wood should be cut away in very early spring just before the blossom appears.

Ash. Little pruning will be required except to shorten excessively long branches.

Beech. This tree makes plenty of twiggy growth which should be cut away each winter otherwise too much sunlight will be kept out of the tree and dead wood will become more plentiful.

Birch. As the silver birch makes height, much of the early twiggy stem growth decays. This must be cut away and it may be necessary to cut back some of the new branch wood should the trees have been planted too closely.

Cerasus. The cherries are now classed with the almond under Prunus. They require no pruning except if making too vigorous growth when they should be root-pruned in preference to branch cutting which will cause gumming. It is several of the Japanese Cherries, Yoshino, Ukon, Kojima, and Jo-nioi which makes very spreading trees and which will possibly require root pruning in later years. Those with an upright habit will require no treatment.

Chestnut. Whilst the Horse Chestnut will require almost no pruning, the Sweet Chestnut will make a better tree if cut back during winter. In fact a row of sweet chestnuts can be made to form a dense screen if kept cut back in alternate years.

Crataegus. The flowering Thorns or May should have all overcrowded and dead wood constantly removed over winter.

Producing a large amount of bloom early in summer it is essential that plenty of light reaches the tree.

Davidia. Little pruning will be required except to thin out weak wood if the tree becomes overcrowded.

Elm. Removal of dead wood which constantly forms, is the main necessity with young elms. With older trees, large branches should be cut back to prevent them snapping off in strong winds.

Hornbeam. The species *pyramidalis*, which makes a fine upright tree may be clipped into shape if it becomes straggling.

Laburnum. These glorious trees tend to make too much woody growth at the centre which should be removed in November if excessive. At the same time dead laterals should be cut away.

Lime. Thinning out the twiggy branch wood will be a necessity and the constant removal of sucker growth formed at the bottom of the trunks.

This is a tree that may be pruned to form a magnificent avenue of espaliers as seen at Chatsworth House. The main stem will form laterals if kept headed back in the same way as for apples and pears. The shoots are trained to wires several feet above the ground.

Mulberry. This is a vigorous growing fruiting tree which to keep it in check should have any new shoots cut back half way during mid-winter.

Oak. The Evergreen Oaks, the Ilex or Holm Oak may be clipped into the required shape in late summer. The Turkey Oak, which like the beech holds its brown, toothed leaves right into winter should have any excess wood removed as becomes necessary. The English Oak, more slow growing will require little pruning except for the removal of excess twiggy wood.

Poplar. This is one plant that must be given constant pruning to keep it within bounds, particularly the Lombardy and Bolleana poplars with their upright habit. To form a screen they should be constantly cut right back to the required height each winter.

The Manchester and balsam scented poplars having a more rounded habit, should be kept in shape by the annual clipping back of vigorous wood. It is possible to cut these trees into a pyramid form thus allowing the maximum of sunlight to reach the centre wood and lower branches.

Prunus. The most popular prunus which are true members of the plum family are the purple leaved species *P. Pissardii* and *P. nigra* both of which bloom in early spring and so should be pruned in early summer after flowering. Dead, twiggy growth must be kept out, but to reduce vigour of the new wood, root pruning is better than too much cutting away of wood.

Pyrus. Flowering in spring and bearing masses of richly coloured fruit in autumn, the crab apples should be pruned during December, cutting away inward branches as the trees become crowded.

Sorbus. In this group is included the Whitebeam and Mountain Ash. Most of the species are slow growing and make little unwanted growth and can be kept in shape by occasional cutting back of new wood in summer.

Walnut. Slow growing except in very rich soils, the tree may be kept in shape by doing any pruning late in summer, cutting away dead wood and cutting back vigorous new shoots.

Willow. All the willows (salix) are rapid growing and may be cut back in early winter to form almost any shape and size. Where the elastic-like shoots are too numerous they should be removed.

CHAPTER VII

CARE AND PRUNING OF HEDGES AND WINDBREAKS

Different pruning treatment for different plants — Arbutus — Beech — Berberis stenophylla — Birch — Box — Buddleia — Conifers — Cotoneaster Franchetti — Escallonia — Gorse — Hazel — Holly — Hornbeam — Hydrangea — Laurel — Lonicera — Olearia — Pear — Pittosporum Mayi — Privet — Pyracantha — Rose — Tamarix — Thuya plicata — Whitehorn — Yew.

Of all the plants in a garden the hedge, no matter of what plants it is comprised, always seems to be the most neglected. Rows of the less hardy plants can be seen devoid of foliage due to frost and cold winds and like this they remain for years. Then there are those hedges which were first planted with good intentions and then for some reason were allowed to grow unchecked and have become so weak and straggling with nothing but old wood at the bottom, that they are almost beyond aid. There is yet another group which comprises a hedge of the suitable but less familiar plants such as the hydrangea and the delightful escallonias, delightful for a hedge but which demand the correct treatment when used in this way, otherwise there will be large gaps caused by the shrubs forming their shoots in an outwards direction rather than sideways, all of which is decided by good pruning.

As a general rule, a hedge will require constant attention when once it has been planted, for subjects like privet, thorn and holly will tend to make much thick, woody growth instead of the desired foliage. This coarse wood will tend to dominate the hedgerow until the only course open will be layering, to persuade the wood to send new shoots in an upwards direction. Layering is a job for a specialist and must be prevented if possible by constant pruning. The familiar subjects such as privet, thorn and beech are quite straightforward in their pruning, this consisting almost entirely of trimming with the shears, but where shrubs of more unruly growth are used, some detailed knowledge of their requirements is essential.

Again, climate must play a large part in the selection and maintainance of a hedge. In the South West, where pittosporum and tamarix grow almost rampant, these plants will need considerable pruning and though they may survive the severe winters of a northern seacoast growth will be very much more restricted and little pruning will be necessary. Soils too, play a large part in the growth of hedging plants and where yew and privet will succeed in a cold, heavy soil, holly and escallonias like a well cultivated loam. Beech favours chalk, spruce a soil of a more acid nature. It all plays a part on pruning. Where possible one should plant an evergreen or at least a plant which retains its berries or tinted leaves until the year end and here I am thinking of cotoneasters and beech.

ARBUTUS. This, the Strawberry Tree, which produces its fruit and blossoms at the same time, will make a tall hedge or screen. Any straggling wood should be cut back in early April.

BEECH and COPPER BEECH. Slow growing but requiring little

pruning other than to remove any dead wood or thick woody shoots by cutting back to persuade them to 'break'.

BERBERIS *stenophylla*. This is a quick growing and graceful member of the family and to build up dense growth at the bottom it should be pruned hard back each March in the same way as for privet.

BIRCH. It is not generally realised that silver birch can be trained to form a delightful hedge if the plants are 'topped' at the required height. But as birch tends to form much dead wood, this should be constantly cut away to make way for new growth.

BOX. Box should never be pruned or clipped until summer, until all risk of cold spring winds has passed, for she doesn't like to be without her winter overcoat too soon. A neglected box hedge should have any old, thick wood cut away when it will 'break' into fresh green shoots.

BUDDLEIA. This plant will make a splendid wind break and should be given more moderate pruning than when used as a shrub. Whilst the plants are becoming established only the dead flower heads should be removed, cutting back to keep the shoot tidy. Then when the tree reaches the required height much of the old wood can be cut out whilst each year after flowering the new wood should be cut back to retain the height. With the arching sprays buddleia makes an attractive screen.

CONIFERS. A number of the evergreen conifers are highly suitable for hedging or a screen, especially *Cupressus Lawsoniana* which will stand pruning to retain shape and height so much better than *C. macrocarpa* which tends to die back after ten years. The silvery *C. Fletcheri* and *C. Potteni* are both valuable and should have the leader shoot cut out at the required height. Future pruning will consist only of keeping top shoots to the necessary height and the removal of any old wood. Conifers will lose too much sap if pruned other than in late autumn.

COTONEASTER *Franchetti*. This is a graceful plant with its grey evergreen foliage and bright orange berries. Any woody growths devoid of foliage should be cut back hard in early April when new growth will be quickly formed during summer.

ESCALLONIA. Magnificent evergreens when used as a hedge in the South and in Coastal areas, but not quite hardy in the exposed North. The arching sprays are covered in bloom from mid-summer until late in autumn. They are best pruned in early March shortening back the flowering shoots and cutting out dead wood. Outward shoots should be cut back almost entirely.

GORSE. The double form is a charming shrub for a windbreak and has a more compact habit than the common single variety. Dead wood should be continually removed and shoots of new wood may be cut back in April.

HAZEL. The Cob and Filbert nut trees make an ideal hedge but should be cut back to retain shape during winter.

HOLLY. When planting a holly hedge it is essential to obtain an often transplanted tree and this should receive no pruning for two years until the roots have become established. A holly hedge should be cut and trained in the wedge-shape to allow the maximum amount of light to reach the base of the plants, otherwise they will become only a mass of decayed wood near the base. Early April is the most suitable time for cutting.

HORNBEAM. This is a good plant for a cold, clay soil, retaining its leaves until well into winter. It requires little thinning or cutting, it only being necessary to retain its shape.

HYDRANGEA. This shrub makes a charming hedge but will require some attention to keep its shape. The faded blooms should be removed, cutting back the new shoots to about half their length to a strong bud. Any dead or surplus wood should be removed each winter.

LAUREL. It is said that a laurel should never be touched with a pair of shears, but should be cut back with a pruning knife in early July to retain its shape and to remove any old wood. An old laurel hedge which has been badly neglected should have the old wood drastically cut down to about 12 inches of the base and from there new growth should be trained to the required height. Drastic pruning is best done early April to allow a full summer for making new growth.

LONICERA, *nitida*. With its tiny glossy foliage and compact habit no better hedge can be planted in the town garden. It may be clipped in the same way as for privet and this should be done in early summer. Also like privet, the plants should be given this attention as soon as planted, to prevent them becoming woody.

OLEARIA. The hardy, evergreen Daisy Bush should be thinned in late August after flowering, removing the flower heads and cutting away any unwanted or dead wood; or where growth is too dense, several of the shoots should be cut back almost to the base in early April.

PEAR. The wild pear makes a splendid field hedge and except for the removal of dead wood and pruning back any over-vigorous shoots, it needs little attention.

PITTOSPORUM *mayi*. This is one of the loveliest of all hedging plants with its black stems and pale crinkly green leaves. It is happiest in the more gentle climate of the South West where it is cut and bunched over winter and sent to Covent Garden, this acting as the only pruning necessary. During summer it throws up its fresh shoots which in turn are cut back over winter.

PRIVET. Hardy in all districts and in all soils both the green and golden types should be cut back each year after planting to enable them to form thick new shoots at the base. A neglected privet, however high, should be cut back to 2 ft. of its base in March. This will cause the old, thick wood to 'break' and it will, within the summer, have covered itself in fresh new growth. A pruning saw will be necessary to cut through the old wood. Any top growth should again be cut back the following early April and the new season's growth cut back half way in early August. Reducing the new top growth and keeping the sides cut back towards the end of each summer will soon see the hedge established again and will see it clothed in green (or gold) before winter.

PYRACANTHA. These delightful evergreens with their glossy leaves and vivid orange berries will soon make a pleasing hedge and if kept cut back each winter after the buds have fallen, they will form plenty of fresh, new wood the following summer.

ROSE. Few realise that for a low hedge there is no lovelier plant than the taller of the polyantha roses, like Alain and August Seebauer; and for a 6 ft. hedge the Moyesi or wild roses are enchanting. The polyanthas should be planted 15 inches apart and after being cut back in March to vigorous buds near the base, they will need little pruning but for the removal of dead and weak wood and cutting away the dead flowers in November. Any strong shoots growing in an outward direction should be cut back to a base bud, for to build up a satisfactory hedge the side shoots should be given preference.

The Moyesi roses make rapid growth and should have their new season's wood cut back half way every March, at the same time cutting away old and weak wood. A species called Fruhlings-gold, which bears double yellow flowers early in summer, also makes a good hedge, for growth is slender and upright and very little attention is necessary apart from cutting away old and weak wood.

TAMARIX. Always at its best near the sea, the feathery foliage makes a most graceful hedge. Any pruning should be done in early spring, cutting back any straggling shoots to shape the hedge and removing any dead wood.

THUYA, *plicata*. This is really a conifer, but so valuable for hedging that it is here given more prominence. It is one of the few conifers, perhaps the only one, which will stand up to severe pruning, for it will quickly make fresh growth on the old wood. Even long neglected trees may be cut back like barren privet and the old wood will sprout just as rapidly as privet. *Thuya vervaeneana*, also evergreen, is more densely growing and may be given the same treatment, but conifers must only be pruned during the resting period, preferably in late autumn or if the situation be unduly exposed, in early spring before the sap begins to rise.

WHITETHORN, or Hawthorn is the most widely planted hedge for a field. The secret of building up a plant of dense growth is to cut back to 9 inches of the base the year after planting, prefer-ably in early spring. Afterwards the hedge should be trimmed into shape with the shears.

A thorn hedge that has been badly neglected is best renovated by layering. All the dead and weak wood is cut away and one or two thick branches or stems are retained. These should be in the same direction to form a continuous row. Stakes are knocked into the ground to keep the branches in position after they have been cut to half way through the stems to enable them to be bent into the required position. A new hedge may therefore be formed from the old wood which will quickly produce fresh growth.

YEW. Because its foliage is poisonous it is not so widely planted, but a well tended yew hedge is unsurpassed as a windbreak and for its beauty. Slow growing, it will require little pruning, merely removing any straggling growth in early spring to retain the shape.

CHAPTER VIII

RENOVATING OLD FRUIT TREES

APPLES AND PEARS

Cutting out dead wood — Pruning young trees — restricting
the vigorous tree — Bark Pruning.

PRUNING an apple tree. It sounds so easy, just as if we should give exactly the same attention to all varieties and use the same methods on a three year old tree as would be done to an old established tree. We discussed in Chapter 1 the need to prune in order to maintain a close connection between a root and top growth and that it would be necessary to first bring the tree gradually into fruiting and then to maintain health and vitality and at the same time attending to such points as the correct ripening of the fruit and how to obtain the best quality fruit from a tree of any age. But let us begin by discussing the care of an old, neglected orchard which the purchaser of an old property so frequently comes up against.

Here the trees may be anything from 20 to 100 years of age. First it will be necessary to see them fruiting so that the various varieties may be given the individual treatment they need. Should you not know the name of all of them, try to send some of the fruit to an apple specialist for identification and then it will be clear as to the first move in the renovating programme. With an old orchard, where the trees are often as tall as a house, a ladder will be necessary to reach most of the branches. But first look at the orchard as a whole, then the individual trees. Don't take the saw and hack off branches here and there just because the trees look untidy. Consider exactly what treatment can be given to each to increase its efficiency.

CUTTING OUT DEAD WOOD

The first operation will be to cut out all dead and decayed wood which is playing no part in the life of the tree and which it will be better without, for the greatest source of disease will then be out of the way. Then look at each tree again and where one branch is possibly growing into another tree causing little light to reach it and obstructing the flow of air around each tree, cut this away also, but when removing any wood, whether decayed or green, make the severance right against the main trunk, and just in the same way if decayed or surplus wood is to

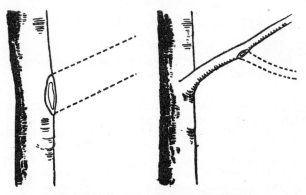

THE REMOVAL OF DECAYED BRANCHES

be removed from a small branch. Frequently it is observed that a branch has been removed an inch or even several inches away from the main trunk or branch with the result that the remaining wood gradually decays and falls a victim to pest and disease, especially Brown Rot Disease which will attack the remaining parts of the tree and also the fruit.

When removing a large branch it is advisable to give it some support whilst the cut is being made to take off much of the weight and so prevent the branch from tearing away from the stem and which would cause considerable damage to the bark.

It will be found that a cut made close to the bark will quite quickly heal over and so will be closed against disease. But it is often noticed with an old orchard that certain branches will have been carelessly removed or may have snapped off leaving several inches of wood which will have decayed and come away leaving an unhealthy looking cavity on the main trunk or on a large branch.

To prevent further decay, this cavity should be filled up with cement or if only a small opening, with putty, but if left untouched there will be the chance that disease may damage the tree past repair.

As I mentioned in Chapter 1, any pruning and de-branching of an old tree must be done by degrees. The first winter, possibly no more than decayed wood and a few small branches overlapping each other will be removed. The following winter more unwanted wood may be cut away, then later if the tree has become exces-

A BRANCH CAREFULLY REMOVED. NEW GROWTH IS BEGINNING TO COVER THE CUT.

sively tall and straggling, it may be advisable to cut back the main branches to a sturdy young shoot and so build up once again the lower part of the tree so that it will in time be capable of bearing a heavy crop. But any rejuvenation of an old, neglected tree must be done gradually. If you take out the saw and pruners and cut away right and left during the first winter there may be nothing but dying trees left. When a tree has been allowed to fall into neglect the temptation to restore its vigour at once, is great, but it must be resisted. It may take four years to renovate an orchard, even longer if the trees are very old.

PRUNING YOUNG TREES

When pruning neglected young trees, large branches will not need to be cut away. Instead, thinning and cutting back laterals to form vigorous buds will be all that is necessary. First remove any overlapping wood, taking care to cut back to an outward bud, for the centre of the tree must be kept as open as possible to let in the maximum of light and air. Then take a careful look at the laterals, which are the shoots growing out from the main stems and on which the fruiting buds are formed. Each season, additional wood is formed and also buds, but if not kept pruned the laterals will become longer and longer and at the same time the buds will become weaker and weaker. Instead of allowing them to remain unchecked with the result that the fruit will be small, they should be cut back to two or three fruiting buds. Into these the energies of the plant will be diverted with the result that the fruit will develop to a good size.

Cutting back the unpruned laterals to two or three buds should be done before the buds begin to swell, in other words before the end of March, in order that when the sap commences to flow it can be directed at once to the fruiting buds and also there will

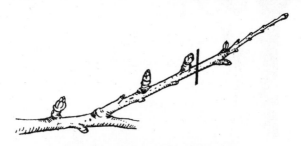

BUILDING STRONG FRUITING BUDS

be a danger of knocking off the buds if pruning is done when they have started to swell. Varieties possessing extreme vigour, such as Bramleys Seedling and Newton Wonder, would be well able to develop four or five buds and too drastic pruning will only increase the vigour of the tree to the detriment of fruit.

RESTRICTING THE VIGOROUS TREE

The very strong growing varieties such as the Worcester Pearmain and Blenheim Orange together with those previously mentioned, will require very little pruning for they do not need any stimulation to make fresh growth. Their growth may of course be regulated by planting a known root-stock of dwarfing habit, but this, of course, is known only where a new tree is being planted. But to prune the vigorous varieties without knowing which they are will cause only disappointment by increasing their wood to the detriment of fruit. Thus it is my contention that no orchard should be touched except to cut away decayed wood without first seeing the trees in fruit.

As it has been seen that to prune hard a vigorous growing tree, will only make it more vigorous, an over-crowded tree of this nature should have a branch or two completely cut away. This will allow the extra light to reach the buds without increasing its vigour. Or it may be restricted by either root or bark pruning. As a rule it may be said that a strong growing tree will form very many less fruit buds than will a slow growing tree and so with the vigorous growers some method of restricting growth will often be necessary. For this reason it is a good idea when planting new trees of vigorous varieties to place a flat stone beneath the tap root to prevent it growing away unrestricted and which would make it more difficult to prune in later years.

November is the best time to root prune and if the tap root is thus checked it will be an easy matter to make a trench 3-4 ft. away from the trunk and to sever the strongest roots, spreading out the fibrous roots before filling in the trench. The same rule of careful pruning, doing only a little at a time apertains equally to the roots as it does to the branches, particularly where old trees are concerned. It is therefore advisable to root prune only one side the first year, the other side the following year. Where standard trees are being grown it is not advisable to remove the tap root which is the tree's anchor. If a stone is used at planting time, the tree will concentrate on strong secondary roots which may if necessary be restricted by pruning.

It should also be remembered that root pruning should be consistent with the removal of wood to retain the balance of the functions of both roots and foliage. In the case of vigorous growers, the removal of a branch or of unwanted wood should correspond to the restriction of roots. In dealing with old wall trees which are being root pruned in order to bring them into full bearing once again, the general practice is to prune back the fruiting spurs at the same time as the roots are cut back and this will ensure quality rather than a quantity of fruits of little value. Thus will the connection between roots and foliage be maintained.

BARK PRUNING

Bark pruning or ringing is done to curb the flow of sap with the result that more fruiting buds are formed instead of wood growth. As there is danger that too much bark may be cut away which would not heal over in a reasonable time, ringing should only be done when root pruning has no effect, but it is worth trying with a tree which refuses to bear a crop and is continually making fresh wood even when every known method of restriction has been tried. Instead of making a complete circle round the stem, it is safer to make two half circles, allowing 6 inches of bark between each. Cutting should be done with a short knife; a pruning knife is best and immediately the cuts have been made and about three-quarters of an inch of bark has been removed, tape should be fastened and bound securely round the place where the cuts were made. Early May is the best time to do this and choose a calm day so that the tissue of the tree at the exposed place is not open to drying winds. Cover with tape immediately each tree has been treated.

PEARS

Everything that has been said about apple trees is much the same for pears, but here again we should discover the name of each tree and learn something of its habits before taking up the pruners. Pears are divided into two sections, those with a vigorous upright habit, and those of a weaker and semi-weeping habit. In the former group are Comice and Durondeau and Clapp's Favourite; of those with slender habit are Louise Bonne and Beurre d'Amanlis. The importance is in pruning for the upright growers to have their buds facing outwards, whilst the slender, weeping growers should be pruned so that the buds, as far as possible face in an upward direction. Most of the weepers are tip bearers and should be pruned but little for they make only a few fruiting buds, but those of vigorous, upright habit may need to have their spurs reduced to obtain fruit of size and quality. The same remarks of the tip bearers in pears also concerns the tip bearers of apples, e.g. Worcester Pearmain, St. Edmund's Russet and Grenadier and these trees will require but little pruning. But every variety should be treated on its merits. Do not over-prune any tree, first try the lightest possible pruning, then wait for the results. Never prune for pruning sake, and a

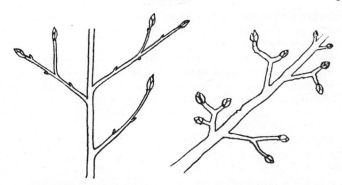

FRUITING BUDS OF A   SPUR BEARING TREE.
TIP BEARING VARIETY.

little at a time is far better, especially with established trees, than being drastic. First look at your trees then try to imagine them in fruit and remember that the aim is a healthy, well balanced tree, one able to bear the maximum amount of the best quality fruit and over as long a period of years as possible.

It should be noticed that each shoot or lateral will form both fruiting and wood or foliage buds, the former being easily distinguished by their habit of appearing on short, woody stems, whilst the wood-making buds lie flat along the stem and are smaller and of a pointed nature.

CHAPTER IX

CARE OF A YOUNG FRUIT TREE

APPLES AND PEARS

Building the framework — The established Spur System —
The Regulated System — The Renewal System — Biennial
Cropping — Branch bending — Notching and Nicking.

In the correct treatment and care of a young fruit tree lies its ultimate cropping powers which include its health, vigour, shape and ability to bear a heavy crop of quality fruit as soon as possible and over as long a period as possible. There is a wide choice of types of tree available; the bush form, standards, cordon, fan-shaped and horizontal trained and each demands rather different treatment not only in its establishment, but in its subsequent care when established. The interesting question of training can be left until the following chapter, but here we are concerned with the care of the young tree after it has been formed.

First it must be remembered that in its early years, a young tree should not be expected to bear excess fruit at the expense of making a healthy frame; at the beginning, the formation of wood is more important than fruit, for a solid and lasting foundation must be formed.

Mr. George Bunyard of Kent always advocated that a newly planted tree, which would be between 2-5 years old, should be allowed to grow away for a full season entirely untouched. This was to allow it to form ample new wood whilst the new roots were forming and so the balance of the tree was left undisturbed. There was then no fear of excessive pruning interfering with the functions of the rooting system whilst settling in.

The following winter, pruning may commence and one should have then formed an idea as to the system to follow. It will be one of three alternatives:—

(a) The Established Spur system, generally carried out for the more artificially trained trees of apples and pears.

(b) The Regulated System which requires the minimum of pruning and which is generally carried out on trees with a vigorous habit, and

(c) The Renewal System, which simplified, means keeping the tree in continuous growth.

THE ESTABLISHED SPUR SYSTEM

The great difference between this system and the older, indiscriminate cutting is to allow the tree a greater freedom of growth with the formation of fruiting spurs along the main branches. Wood formed during the summer is cut back during winter to four buds. During the following summer the two top buds will make new growth whilst the lower spurs will develop into fruiting buds. From the place above the top buds where the cut has been made, two laterals will have formed during the second season, which in turn are cut back (B) to two buds. Thus after two seasons you have this:—

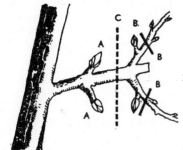

FORMING A FRUIT SPUR.

This method will ensure that whilst the tree is concentrating its energies to the formation of fruiting spurs at (A), the balance of the tree is being maintained with the spurs forming fruiting buds without having to form new growth themselves.

During the third winter, the fruiting spurs being now correctly formed, the previous year's wood is cut back (at C), for its functions are now complete and the energies of the tree can concentrate on the production of fruit at the two spurs (A). Again to encourage the building up of a strong fruiting spur, the laterals should be pinched back during mid-summer, reducing them by about a third. In this way a tree is built up to its full fruit-bearing capacities in the quickest possible time, bearing in mind the affinity between the rooting system and the formation of foliage, both necessary to maintain the vigour and health of the tree. When once the tree is established, little pruning will be necessary other than to remove any overcrowded branches and to cut out all overcrowded spurs. This method is of course suitable only for the spur-bearing varieties such as Cox's Orange Pippin, Christmas Pearmain, etc., and it is the trained forms which generally respond to this method the best. The method of thinning the fruiting spurs has been described in Chapter VIII, exactly the same as for old-established trees.

A word should be said about the necessity to thin out the spurs when once the trees have become established, when they are about ten years old, and those taking over a garden with trees of this age should remember that if no spur thinning is done the tree may soon exhaust itself by forming excess fruit, too much for it to carry in comparison with tree growth. Most gardeners are shy at removing fruiting buds, but in any case too many will cause a reduction in the size and quality of the fruit.

The spurs may be cut back at A or the upper section of buds may be left untouched and the whole of the lower spur removed at B. Both would have the desired effect of the tree concentrating its energies to but 4 or 5 buds as against double the number.

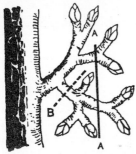

TREATMENT OF AN ESTABLISHED SPUR.

The question of the tip bearers does not come into this system for in any case they are not suitable for training in the artificial forms.

THE REGULATED SYSTEM

This system is more suitable for the tip bearers and for bush and standard trees of all apples and pears, for these are the most natural forms of fruiting trees. By using vigorous rootstocks like Malling II for apples and Quince A for pears, the tree will not come into bearing as quickly as if the dwarfing rootstocks are used, but it will retain its vigour and its fruiting capacities over a much longer period. With the tip bearers any excessive pruning will cause greatly diminished cropping, for the buds are borne at the end of the laterals and not in clusters as with the spur bearers. So under this system cut away as much over-crossing and centre wood as to keep the tree 'open' and also remove all in-growing laterals as they are observed each season. Any strongly growing branches which appear to be growing away too quickly should be cut back, or de-horned as it is called, to a lateral growing out in a manner that will encourage the shape of the tree. The spur bearers should have their spurs thinned out in the way previously described and though this will not be so essential as with those trees growing on a dwarf rootstock or in artificial forms, over-crowded spurs should be regularly thinned. This system demands just as constant attention in the pruning programme and a little cutting back should be done each year, rather than the removal

5. Cordon Gooseberries, correctly trained and pruned and bearing a heavy crop.

Photo: George Pyne.

6.
Moderate pruning of a Rose bush. Weakly wood has been removed.

Photo: R. A. Malby & Co.

7. An established bush apple which has been carefully pruned. Note the spurs which have received careful attention.

8. A nicely pruned black currant.

of excessive wood in alternate years. Those varieties which are excessively strong growing should be root pruned every three or four years for if too much de-horning is done this may only increase the vigour and too much wood will be the result to the detriment of fruit.

When forming new fruit trees, the less pruning the better until the fruiting buds have started to form, for pruning tends to encourage excess wood at the expense of fruiting buds. So first allow the trees a full year's growth before pruning, then commence with the bush and standard forms by shortening back the new season's wood of the leaders by a third at the end of every season. Then as the tree begins to take shape the leaders will require only tipping each year and possibly occasional de-horning if growth is too vigorous. The laterals too, for spur bearers will require cutting back as described, the tip bearers being left untouched until the time when they become excessive and some wood may have to be cut away.

THE RENEWAL SYSTEM

This works out exactly as described; it is the continual renewal of old wood by new thus retaining the vigour of the tree over a very long period without making too much old wood. The idea is to maintain a balance between the production of new wood and fruit buds and so it is necessary to build up an open tree with well-spaced, erect branches for it is on these that the new wood is continually formed. Suitable erect growing shoots or leaders which form on these branches are pruned back to form replacement branches which in due course will take the place of the older branches. The same method takes place with side shoots. These are left to fruit unpruned. They are then cut back to within two buds of the base which will then produce two more shoots. Again, these are left unpruned and allowed to fruit. In turn, each of the two shoots are pruned back to two buds after fruiting and so the process of the continual replacement of new wood for old goes on. The proportion of shoots pruned and left untouched will be governed by the vigour of the variety. For Bramley's Seedling a better balance will be maintained if a greater proportion of shoots are left unpruned, for stimulation is not required. But much will depend on the general health and vigour of the variety or tree. If the tree seems to be making heavy weather of life, it will require more pruning of side growths to provide the necessary stimulation. Where a tree is healthy and vigorous a large number of the shoots may be left unpruned for as long as three or four years, thus maintaining a balance between fruit and wood.

BIENNIAL CROPPING

In Chapter I we mentioned the value of pruning to regulate cropping and of timing the fruit as in the case of autumn raspberries. With apples there is a tendency for certain varieties, e.g., Blenheim Orange, Miller's Seedling and Newton Wonder, to form an extremely heavy crop in alternate seasons and some form of regulated pruning is necessary to limit the blossom during the 'on' year so that the fruit will retain its size and to encourage the tree to bear a certain amount the following, or 'off' year. All spurs should be reduced to two buds and all maiden wood must be left unpruned. This will ensure that blossom buds will be numerous for the following season whilst during the 'on' year, much of the vigour of the tree will be utilised in the formation of new buds rather than on the concentration of those already formed. Where possibly severe frost has damaged the blossom for one year it frequently happens that the tree will produce an excessive amount of fruit the following year and this may be followed by a lean year. By employing these methods a more regular crop will be assured.

A variety expected to make a good-sized fruit very early in the season, such as Grenadier and Emneth Early apples; and pear Doyenné d'Eté, it will be necessary to cut back their laterals more than is normally done. Instead of cutting back a third of the wood, as much as two-thirds will ensure a more rapid maturing of the fruit even if the quantity may not be so high as when given normal treatment.

BRANCH BENDING

Where a tree is making such excessive growth that there is a fear that further pruning will only stimulate more wood, branch or shoot bending will help to halt this and at the same time by restricting the flow of sap will help to form fruit buds at the expense of new wood. It is the lower branches which are more easily bent and they may be either tied at their tips to the stem of the tree or may be weighted down with strong stones or bricks fastened with cord to their tips. Whilst this does not really come under the title of pruning it does restrict growth of fresh wood and will also cause these bent branches to bear a heavy crop of fruit. In this way, old fruiting shoots can be constantly replaced by new wood.

NOTCH

NOTCH TO RETARD A BUD

NOTCHING AND NICKING

It often happens that a certain bud is required to be restricted in its growth whilst another may refuse to break and so may cause the tree to become mis-shapen. To encourage a bud to break, a notch should be made above it and to retard a bud, a notch should be made on the stem immediately beneath it shaving off a small piece of bark.

BUD

In general it is found that the most vigorous buds are those towards the top of a stem or branch, the vigour diminishing with the buds at the centre and being less vigorous at the lowest point. It may therefore be necessary to stimulate those at the lowest point by notching and this would even out the formation of branches.

Nicking of the stem has a similar effect. It is generally done where restriction of the extension of lateral growth is required. In addition to the cutting back of the stem, the prevention of an extension by the top bud will ensure that those buds lower down the branch will make more growth which may be the object when building up a bush or standard tree. The cut or nick should be made with a sharp knife.

CHAPTER X

TRAINING YOUNG TREES

APPLES AND PEARS

Value of trained Trees — Bush and Standard Forms — Dwarf
Pyramids — Cordons — Horizontal form.

THERE is no more interesting occupation than in training and
building up a young fruit tree so that it will bear a heavy crop on
branches so formed that the tree will prove most economical in
the position in which it is to be planted. In a small garden,
possibly one enclosed by a wall, wall-trained trees may be so
formed that they will bear a useful crop of quality fruit without
occupying more than a few feet of space. There are varieties
suitable for growing against a North wall such as Lord Derby
and James Grieve apple or Pitmaston Duchess pear and of course
almost all will be happy against a South wall.

Then there is the horizontal trained tree, so valuable for planting along a path or around a lawn, whilst the cordon is ideal
for the very small garden, bearing a heavy crop in a restricted
space and coming quickly into bearing. But those of more
natural form will require just as careful handling throughout and
will need to be trained for both health, vigour, and cropping
capabilities in the same way. The various types may be divided
into sections all needing different treatment in the formation of the
tree, but all responding to similar methods of pruning when
established. They are:—

(a) Bush and standard forms.
(b) Dwarf Pyramid.
(c) Cordons.
(d) Espalier or horizontal.
(e) Fan-shaped.

BUSH AND STANDARD FORMS

Let us take the Bush and Standard forms first for they will
require much the same treatment and present few difficulties.

Apples in the bush form should always be purchased as
'maiden' trees which are simply one year old for they may then be
brought along as it is desired right from the infant stage. For a
standard, what is called a two-year feathered tree should be
obtained, for besides its quickness to become established, it may
be trained to the length of stem required. 'Feathers' are the small

lateral shoots on the main stem or trunk. The tree should be allowed to grow away without any check or pruning, then when the standard has reached its desired height it should have its 'feathers' removed and the head is then built up in the same way as for a bush tree.

Formation will consist of two methods:—

(a) The Open Centre form, and
(b) The delayed Open Centre.

It is the Open Centre form which is generally employed and this is obtained by removing the main lateral or stem possibly to as much as 18 inches. From just below this cut, sturdy laterals are formed which will become the main branches of the tree. These should be allowed to grow away for two years when they may be tipped to persuade them to 'break' along the stems. Any laterals or feathers which may appear down the lower portion of the stem should be cut back half way each year and finally removed altogether as soon as the head has taken shape.

The Delayed Open Centre tree is formed by removing only the very top 4-6 inches of the main stem. Then down the whole length buds are formed and it is from these that the tree is built up. So as not to interfere with the laterals which will grow from the top two buds, the two immediately beneath should be removed. This will prevent the centre from becoming crowded. With this form it is the spacing that is all important and to see that the shoots are facing in the right direction on all sides of the tree rather than too many appearing together.

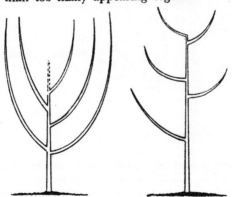

OPEN CENTRE FORM.   DELAYED OPEN CENTRE FORM.

Remember that those trees with a dwarf rootstock and of weaker habit will require more vigorous pruning of the laterals than those varieties of more vigorous habit. The tree is then subjected to one of the systems outlined in the previous chapter.

DWARF PYRAMIDS

This is a form of great value in the small garden and which can be built up into a heavy cropping tree in as short a period as possible. As it is desired to make as much growth as possible at the beginning and the tree to be brought into bearing early, bud growth must be stimulated. This is done by making a cut in the bark just above each of the buds on the main stem taking care to select buds suitably spaced. These shoots may be pruned back to half the new season's growth each year so as to stimulate the formation of fruiting buds, and all blossom buds forming on the leader should also be removed. The dwarfing East Malling rootstock Type II should be selected and vigorous trees should not be chosen for dwarfing forms. When once the tree comes into bearing it should be thinned out as for other forms by using one of the proven systems of pruning. Throughout its early life and until thoroughly established the main or central extension shoot must be constantly pruned back so that the tree can concentrate its energies on the formation of branches.

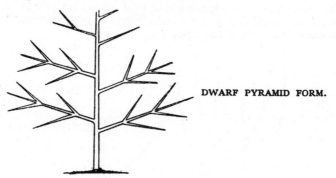

DWARF PYRAMID FORM.

CORDONS

It is the single stemmed cordon that is most frequently used and which should be planted at an oblique angle so as to limit its tendency to grow away. Once again, a dwarfing rootstock should be used and neither a vigorous tree like the Bramley nor a tip bearer like the Worcester Pearmain. Likewise the upright spur bearers of pears should only be used. The maiden trees should be planted 3 ft. apart and should be fastened to wires at an angle of 45°. The extension or main stem is never pruned and in the early years pruning consists of cutting back the laterals during August to 6 inches from the main stem. This summer pruning will ensure the formation of fruiting spurs as quickly as possible. When the tree has made the necessary growth, the leader may be cut back so that the tree can concentrate on the formation of fruit rather than on extending its form. Henceforth the tree may be kept healthy and the fruit of a high quality by the careful elimination of surplus spurs and a tree with excessive vigour may be curbed with root pruning done every three years. But by keeping the stem at an oblique angle this will also retard the formation of too much new wood.

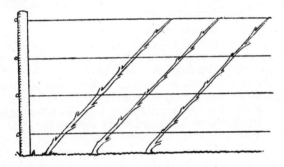

Besides the Single or Oblique cordon, the U-shaped form, or Double cordon should be understood as this is occasionally required. Though growing in an upwards direction as against the angle of the single cordon, the bend at the bottom will act as a check to vigorous growth. The U-cordon will be grown against a wire frame as in the case of espaliers and single cordons. Its formation is in fact very similar to that of the horizontal trained tree, the maiden being cut back to 12 inches of stem to two buds facing in opposite directions. These are allowed to grow unpruned throughout the year being fastened to canes against the wires, first at an angle, then gradually to a vertical position.

Pruning consists of cutting back the leaders each autumn to one-third of their new season's growth and of pinching out any side growth during August. These side shoots may be further cut back in November to two buds which will form the fruiting spurs. A variety showing excessive vigour may be root pruned in alternate years. Should either of the buds fail to form an arm, notching or nicking immediately above will have the desired stimulating effect.

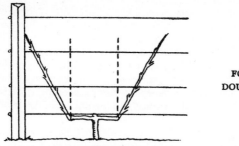

FORMING THE
DOUBLE CORDON.

ESPALIER OR HORIZONTAL FORM

Trained horizontally along the wires in a similar position as for cordons, there is no more satisfying way of growing apples and pears adaptable to this form. A maiden should always be planted, the stem being shortened to about 18 inches above soil level and to a point where there are two buds close together, one on either side of the stem. It is a simple matter to train the tree, the laterals formed by the two buds being tied to the wires to the right and to the left, whilst the extension shoot is allowed to grow away unchecked until sufficient growth has been made for it to be cut back to two more buds similarly placed and spaced about 15-18 inches above the first to form. To encourage more rapid growth, the laterals should first be fastened at the angle of 45° and only placed in the horizontal position at the end of the first year's growth. Small canes should be used to train it at this angle otherwise there will be fear of damage by strong winds.

A new tier may be formed each season and when the first has been formed, to encourage it to form fruiting spurs, all shoots formed on these branches should be pruned back in summer to within 5 inches of the main stem. This will encourage the plant to form fruiting buds instead of new wood. The work should be done towards the end of July. This is followed by cutting back still further during winter in the usual way. Treatment then consists of thinning out the established spurs, and root pruning if the tree is inclined to make excessive growth. As the side arms

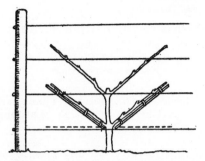

TRAINING TO THE
HORIZONTAL FORM

continue to make wood, this new wood should be shortened back
to a half of the newly formed wood each winter, again making
certain to cut to a bud which is to form the extension shoot. This
may continue for a number of years and until the branches reach
the required number. To make for ease in picking and pruning,
it is general to allow five pairs of arms or tiers to form the top at a
height of about 7 ft.: the reach of the average man.

It sometimes happens that a bud will fail to 'break' which
would mean the loss of an arm and a badly balanced plant. In
order to persuade the bud into growth, a notch should be made
immediately above the bud, a small piece of bark being removed.
This will stimulate the bud into growth.

NOTCHING TO STIMULATE A BUD

FAN TRAINED

As it is almost only the stone fruits which are grown in this way,
pears being grown against a wall in the horizontal fashion, this
method will be described in the following Chapter XI.

TREATMENT AND PRUNING OF STONE FRUITS

Plums — Spring Pruning — Root Pruning — Treatment of
the Fan trained tree — Forming the Fan Shaped tree —
Cherries — Morello cherries — Peaches and Nectarines —
Apricots.

UNDER this heading come Peaches and Nectarines, Plums and
Sweet Cherries, with the Acid Cherries requiring the same
treatment as the peaches and nectarines.

PLUMS. Spring is the best time to carry out any pruning of
plums, just when the buds are beginning to burst for it is at this
time that the wounds quickly heal over and almost no 'bleeding'
occurs. This not only reduces the vigour of the tree but provides
an entrance for the dreaded Silver Leaf disease, the fungus deriv-
ing its nourishment from the cells of the tree, thereby greatly
decreasing its constitution. Early autumn pruning, which may be
carried out on early fruiting varieties when the crop has been
cleared, is permissible, but all cutting should be done between
the end of April and mid-September for during winter the cuts
will remain 'open' for dangerously long periods.

In any case, plums require very little pruning, for the trees
will form their fruit buds throughout the whole length of the
younger branches and especially with standard trees which are
established; thinning of overcrowded growth either in May or
September, depending upon lateness of crop, will be all that is
required. A well-grown plum tree will be able to carry a much
larger proportion of wood than will any other fruit tree and
drastic reduction, even of neglected trees, must never be
performed as with apples and to a lesser extent, pears.

When renovating a neglected tree, it may be advisable to cut
away with the pruning saw one or two large and partially decayed
branches. If so, this should be done during May, a time when the
large cut will heal rapidly and so that the energies of the tree may
be concentrated to the remaining wood. With plums it is even
more important to cut out any wood close to the stem from which
it is being removed so that the wound will heal rapidly and
completely. But before making any cuts, see if the tree can be
renewed in vigour by removing some of the small, thin wood
which plums make in quantity and possibly root pruning will be
more satisfactory than the cutting back of any large branches.

Root Pruning

One of the greatest troubles with plums is the continual formation of suckers at the roots which if left will utilise much of the
nourishment needed for the proper functioning of the tree. These
should be removed whenever the roots of the tree are pruned and
must be cut away right from their source otherwise they will
continue to grow again. It is first necessary to remove the soil
from around the tree to expose the roots, but it will be found that
the suckers generally arise from a point in the roots just below the
point where the scion has been grafted on to the rootstock. This
calls for the utmost care in removing the soil right up to the scion
and then in cutting out the sucker shoots with a sharp knife. For
bush or standard trees it is advisable to ring round half the tree
one year and to complete the removal of suckers and vigorous
roots the following year. It is essential to pack the soil well round
the roots when the work has been done or there will be the
chance of the tree becoming uprooted by strong winds.

Treatment of Fan Trained Trees

In renovating fan trained trees, in which form the plum crops
abundantly, more pruning will be necessary and this should take
the form of pinching back shoots in mid-summer and in removing
completely all unwanted new wood. A number of young growths
may be pinched back between mid-June and mid-July to form a
new spur system and these will need to be cut further back, in the
same way as described for apples, but early in September rather
than in winter. Then by degrees the old spurs may be drastically
reduced to make way for the new ones. In conjunction with the
shoot thinning of wall trees, root pruning should be given every
three or four years which will prevent excessive wood growth.

The formation of a bush and standard form of plum tree takes
the same lines as described for apples and pears. Planted in the
maiden form they may be formed as required, the yearly pruning
consisting of pinching back the new wood to form fruiting buds.

Forming the Fan Trained Tree

Both plums and cherries crop abundantly in this form, all
varieties proving suitable, though naturally some are more
vigorous than others and will require more frequent pruning at
the roots. The method of forming the fan is to cut back the
maiden to an upward bud. This should leave on the lower portion
of the stem two buds which will break and form the arms.

Unsuitably placed buds should be removed and any not breaking must be nicked or notched as previously described for the formation of espaliers.

After the previous season's growth, they are pruned back to 18 inches and the leader or central shoot is cut back to two buds. It is from these buds that the fan shaped tree is formed.

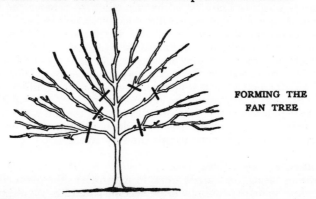

FORMING THE FAN TREE

Canes are used for tying in the shoots so that they may be trained to the required shape. As growth continues, each shoot may be cut back the following spring to two more buds which will complete the shape of the tree, though canes will be needed until the shoots have taken on the required form.

Cultural treatment will henceforth consist of cutting back a third of the new wood formed by the branches each May and the pinching back of all side growths. The shoots will continue to break and where there is room a number may be tied in to continue the fan-like shape.

CHERRIES. Being much slower growing, the cherry will make considerably less growth than the plum and so will need less pruning. This is all to the good for the serious 'bleeding' or gumming of the cherry where cut, will sap its energy and also like the plum will be a source for Silver Leaf infection. August seems to be the best time for any pruning, after the crop has been gathered. All dead, or those branches interfering with each other, should be cut away and where any dense growth has been made, which may not be until the tree is 20 years old, this should be thinned out.

In the case of the fan-trained tree, it is only the side growths which should be removed, pinching back to about six leaves late in June and then further pinching back to four buds early in September. If it is noticed that the main leaders are making excessive growth, rather than cut them and cause further stimulation, they will respond better to the bending down of the shoots for a period of twelve months bringing them forward from the wall and tying the tips against the main stem. This will weaken growth and they may be pruned and tied back in their normal position in 12-18 months. Root pruning as described will do much to keep the cherry in check.

MORELLO CHERRIES. This apertains to the management of the sweet cherry; the Morello or acid cherry requires a different treatment. Acid or sour cherries, like peaches and nectarines, bear their fruit on the previous season's wood and so the aim must be to encourage a continual supply of new wood. For this, the laterals should be cut back half way each autumn, then in spring all side growths should be cut or pinched back to two inches of growth. The previous season's shoots should now be bearing both new wood and blossom buds and it is upon these that the present year's fruit is borne. At the base will be found several buds which should be removed to leave but a single bud which will continue to make new growth through the summer for fruiting next season. Like the sweet cherries and plums, the Morellos can be allowed to carry plenty of wood without fear of reducing the amount of fruit, so thinning is not so necessary and should be done only when need arises. Root pruning will help to keep wall trees in check. As the acid cherries are prone to Brown Rot Disease, all diseased wood when observed must be carefully removed.

PEACHES AND NECTARINES. Whether grown indoors as a fan-trained tree or against a South wall in the open, these stone fruits will require similar pruning as will acid cherries, they bear their fruit on the new season's growth which must be encouraged to form.

During May, new growth formed by the leaders should be cut back by about one-third, whilst the tips of the side growths should be pinched out during mid-summer, pinching them back when they are about 2 inches long. At the base of these shoots, will be retained a single wood bud to grow on as a replacement for next season's fruit, the shoot which has fruited being removed at the end of the season.

In the early years of the tree, pruning should take the same lines as for the renewal system for apples; that is, whilst the tree is being built up, the shoot which will have borne fruit being allowed to grow on until it has reached about 18 inches. This is then fastened to the wall and the tip pinched back to a wood bud. It is the shoot formed from this bud that will bear the next season's crop.

 (*a*) REPLACEMENT SHOOT.
 (*b*) SIDE GROWTHS PINCHED BACK.
 (*c*) LEADER GROWING AWAY.

It frequently happens that when building up a fan-shaped peach, that the branches or arms on one side are more vigorous than those of the other side. This should not be allowed to go unchecked otherwise the balance of the tree will be completely spoilt. As it is known that the branches of the more horizontal shoots are less vigorous than those of a more vertical position, the shoots of the weaker side should be moved to a more vertical position whilst those on the more vigorous side should be fastened back more horizontally. In this position they should remain until growth has become more even.

It is not a difficult matter to distinguish between blossom and wood buds, the latter are small and pointed, whilst blossom buds are round and fat. Where possible select a wood bud facing the wall for an extension shoot for this will ensure a straighter shoot.

Peaches and Nectarines will require more space in which to bear new wood than will either plums or sweet cherries.

Peaches grown as bush trees should be drastically pruned back in early May each year to encourage a continuous supply of new growth. This will stimulate growth which is excessive and should be retarded by ringing round the roots and cutting back in alternate years after the establishment of the trees.

The chief source of worry is the tendency of the plant to 'bleed' or 'gum', but this will not prove troublesome if too much old wood is not allowed to form. This, when pruned is most likely to 'gum', so it is advisable to encourage as much new wood as possible.

All shoots appearing next to a fruit should be pinched out above the second leaf. This removal of all unwanted shoots should be spread out over a period of 3-4 weeks early in summer.

APRICOTS. Again, the fan-trained tree is most suitable for the apricot, replacement shoots being formed in the same way, but it bears its fruit on short spurs which should not be cut back. The apricot also fruits on the preceding season's growth and as soon as the old spurs have borne fruit for two seasons, they should be cut back to make way for newly formed spurs. Side shoots should be pinched back to 1 inch of the stem during summer whenever they form, otherwise the tree will be carrying too much growth and the fruit will suffer in consequence.

CHAPTER XII

PRUNING THE VINE AND FIG

THE VINE

The Vine — Alternative Pruning Methods — Growing Indoors — The Long Rod System — The Spur System — Outdoor Cultivation — Figs — Pruning for Fruit — Root Pruning.

I HAVE grown vines outdoors in the sheltered districts of the South West and as far North West as Lancashire; and in a completely cold greenhouse in Scotland and have found them an easy and most interesting crop. That they are not planted more freely would seem to be in no small measure due to their pruning needs, which many seem to think present the greatest difficulties.

But first it would be better to consider the nature of a vine for there are various ways of pruning. The vine is capable of making considerable fresh growth during a season, a young shoot often reaching a length of 20 ft. or more. If this is cut back to half its growth, it is then called a rod and on this grapes may be borne the following year. In fact, every eye may develop a shoot which will be capable of bearing a bunch or two of grapes. But at the same time buds appearing on the older wood or rods are also capable of bearing fruit, but should there be a preponderance of new wood, then those eyes formed on the old rods will not find sufficient vigour to form. A vine, however well grown cannot be expected to bear fruit in plenty on both the new and old wood so one has the choice either of:—

(a) Allowing one or two new roots to make considerable growth and restricting all other new growth. This is known as the long rod system, or

(b) Allowing the plant to bear a larger number of growths, but keeping these shortened, or

(c) Cutting back all new wood to the main stem to form the spur system.

INDOOR GROWING

The Long Rod System

All pruning with the vine must be performed in winter, during the dormant period before the sap begins to rise. New Year's

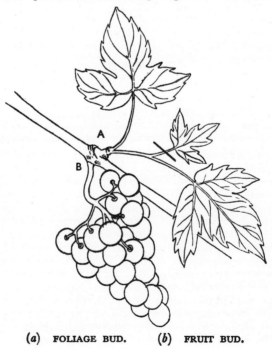

(a) FOLIAGE BUD.   (b) FRUIT BUD.

Day is generally chosen by the specialist growers to begin pruning, but all work should end by the first day or so of February. With a new vine indoors, it is found most suitable to form two main stems or rods which are trained in an outward direction and which are allowed to grow at will during their first year. During this time they will make around 20 ft. of growth and at the year end one of them, the weakest, is cut back to two eyes at the base. As with fruiting trees the important point to keep constantly in mind is the close connection between root activity and the formation of new wood which means that the plant should be allowed to make as much leaf as can be properly maintained.

The remaining shoot should be tied to the roof for it is on this that next season's crop will be borne, whilst the stronger of the two buds should be trained to bear next season's wood and crop whilst the original may in turn be cut back to two eyes, the stronger of which should be retained for growing on. This is known as the long rod system (a).

To prevent overcrowding all laterals must be cut back to two buds, one of which will bear the fruit and the other which should be stopped at two leaves to provide the nourishment.

If in excess, some foliage should be removed.

The Spur System

Not nearly so commonly used, is the short spur system. From the rod which has been allowed to grow away unchecked during the first year, alternate buds are selected on each side of the stem to produce short laterals the following season. These bear fruit and are stopped one joint beyond. The shoots are then cut back to two buds in winter. The rod is not removed, but from one of the two eyes fruit and leaf growth forms the following year.

But the most popular method is now the established spur system. A newly planted vine is cut back to two eyes or buds which are trained up the roof in opposite directions. For the first year they are allowed to grow at will. The following winter they are cut back to half their length and all laterals are cut back to two buds one of which as we have seen will produce fruit, the other leaf. This will eventually build up a system of spurs similar to those of spur bearing apples.

All fruit bearing laterals should be stopped at the first joint after the bunch has formed and all non-fruiting laterals must be pinched back to but 2 inches. All unwanted laterals should be removed completely.

The one drawback to the established spur system is that old vines are frequently found to be a mass of spurs, far too many for the formation of a yield of quality fruit. Where this is the case a number of the spurs should be cut right away, using a sharp knife, for on an average one lateral shoot to every foot length of rod is sufficient. All laterals should be cut back to the first good eye or bud from the main rod.

With an established vine it frequently happens that with the commencement of a new season, those buds situated at the lower

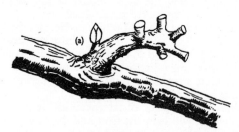

OLD SPUR PRUNED TO ONE BUD (*a*) FOR NEW SEASON'S LATERAL.

portion of the rods refuse to make any growth, whilst those at the rods are most vigorous. To even out this growth, the rods should be lowered from the roof for several weeks before being tied back again. This will persuade the lower buds to break whilst at the same time retarding those at the top.

During the first season the vine should not be allowed to bear any fruit and each lateral should be allowed to bear only a single bunch during the following two seasons.

With the pinching of laterals during summer, this should be done over a period of several days so as not to cause any check to the growing plant which too vigorous defoliation may do. Then later, all lateral growths formed from the shortened non-fruiting lateral must be pinched back as soon as they have made one leaf so as to concentrate the plants' energies into the forming of fruit.

OUTDOOR GROWING

Though we occasionally see a vine growing in the open against a sunny wall in the usual vertical position of the greenhouse, it is rarely we see them in the horizontal form which suits them so much better. They require exactly the same treatment as for espalier pears. First a young plant is cut back during winter to the three lowest buds about 15 inches from the ground, the cut being made immediately above a bud growing in an upwards direction. This is to form a leader shoot. The buds beneath should be trained, one on one side and one on the other, first in an upright position, then when growth becomes vigorous the rods may be tied to wires in a horizontal position. At the end of the season these rods should be shortened back; also the leader shoot. The following season other rods, spaced 15-18 inches above, should be trained in the same way. Each rod or arm is treated in the same way, as for the indoor spur method. All buds on the lower side of the arms or rods should be rubbed out.

Vines grown in the open in the vertical position may either be grown against a wall or trained up stakes or wires just like runner beans. In this way, they would follow the single rod and spur system, all laterals being pinched back as described for indoor vines.

FIGS

Requiring similar temperatures and conditions to the vine, the fig is always happiest near the coast where even as far north as

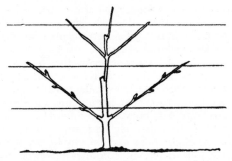

STARTING THE HORIZONTAL VINE AT A 45° ANGLE.

North Wales they can be expected to bear an abundance of fruit. Again, like the vine, figs bear the heaviest crops on horizontal branches and yet it is almost always in the vertical position that they are seen. Perhaps, to compromise, the low fan shaped method may be employed, the trees being formed as described in Chapter XI.

PRUNING FOR FRUIT

As the fruit is produced on the new season's wood the only pruning that can be given an established tree is to limit the shoots which will be produced from each fruit bud. The replacement shoot should be stopped at about the fourth leaf and this should be done at the end of July. Too early cutting back will upset the balance of the tree, for the fruit to mature the following summer will form too quickly and at the expense of both wood and root formation, yet at the same time if the shoot is not pinched back the fruit will not develop and will turn yellow and fall.

The fruits form at the axils of the leaves and will remain until the following spring when they will commence to swell. If extension shoots are pinched back towards the end of July, new fruitlets will form at the axil of each leaf and these will be next season's crop.

Much of the old wood and its extension shoot may remain each season, but if the tree becomes overcrowded some of the wood that carried the previous season's fruit will have to be cut away. The size of the area to be covered and the vigour of the tree will decide as to what wood should be retained.

ROOT PRUNING

Should the tree show excessive new growth, root pruning will be necessary and a too vigorous habit is frequently a cause of trouble with the fig. If the plant makes excessive growth, then fruit bearing will be limited. To keep the plant in check it may be necessary to root prune in alternate years by removing the soil 3 ft. away from the stem and severing the thickest of the roots. It is then advisable to fill in the trench with lime rubble and crushed stone, rammed well down. This will help to restrict the vigorous roots should they have been planted in the open ground rather than in large pots buried in the border.

Figs growing under glass may be made to bear two crops in a single season. If slight heat can be employed, the figs formed during the previous season will commence to swell in early spring if the extension shoots are stopped at the fourth leaf. The fruit that forms throughout spring and whilst the first crop is reaching maturity late in May, will in its turn reach maturity about mid-August. Again, the shoots formed during the latter part of summer will be those on which the fruitlets will form for the crop the following spring. As new growth is formed more profusely with indoor figs, much of the older wood should be cut away each winter.

CHAPTER XIII

PRUNING AND TRAINING SOFT FRUITS

Pruning to lengthen the life of a fruiting bush — Black
Currants — Red Currants — The Gooseberry — Raspberries
—The Loganberry — The Blackberry and Hybrid Berries —
Japanese Wineberry.

THE purpose of training and pruning soft fruits is to get them to
bear the maximum amount of fruit in the most economical area
of ground and over the longest possible period, which means that
the health of the tree must be considered equally with its cropping
powers. This especially is necessary in the case of gooseberries
and currants, unpruned trees giving a heavy crop at first, but
when the tree becomes a mass of dead wood, cropping becomes
lighter each year and the tree is eventually abandoned, either
dug up or cut back to wood which has lost all powers of rejuvenation. A gooseberry should remain vigorous and prolific for
nearly half a century. Likewise black currants; most gardens
possess a few long neglected bushes which are bearing a light crop
in proportion to the amount of ground they occupy. Here too,
judicious pruning would work wonders. Then there are the cultivated hybrid berries, some of which bear their fruits on the old
cane as well as on the new, others on new wood only and it is
advisable to know just what to cut away and when, otherwise
there will be, in a very short time, nothing but a mass of old cane
carrying very little fruit.

The question of regulating fruiting must also be decided by
pruning in the case of autumn fruiting raspberries. Pruning at
the wrong time will seriously harm the crop. Of all plants soft
fruits respond to careful pruning more than any others.

BLACK CURRANTS. Early November is the ideal time to prune,
new shoots being encouraged to form at the base and these should
replace the older wood, the process being continuous throughout
the life of the plant which should be considerable if this regular
pruning is performed. A number of extra vigorous shoots may also
be cut back to promote a shapely tree, but unlike red currants
the spurring back of wood is not done. On inspection it will be
found that whereas the black currant makes long cane-like
growth from the base, the red currant makes spur-like growth, the
wood being made on laterals or branches carried on a 'leg'. It
should also be realised that the black currant bears its fruit right

81

down the stem, whereas the red currant forms its grape-like bunches of fruit at the base of the lateral wood. It is essential to understand the form of the various fruits before contemplating any pruning, it is not a question of just cutting out wood for the sake of it or to make the plant look tidy. Again to give no pruning will be to reduce the vigour of the bush. What is required is "new wood for old" and new wood cannot be formed if too much old wood remains. Producing their new growth from buds beneath soil level, black currants cannot be trained into artificial forms. If the garden is small a variety with a less vigorous habit, like the late fruiting Amos Black, should be selected.

When planting a young black currant, the shoots should be cut back to 6 inches of the base of each stem. This will encourage new shoots to form the following summer which will bear fruit the next year.

RED CURRANTS. For an established bush, old wood is not required to be cut away for the fruit is borne at the base of the laterals, in spur-like form. The new laterals are cut back to half their length each season whilst a shapely bush is built up. Later, to make room for new growth it will be advisable to cut away some of the oldest wood.

When planting a young red (or white) currant, prune back the laterals to two buds. These will form strong laterals the following summer and these in turn should again be cut back to two buds during winter and so the process continues.

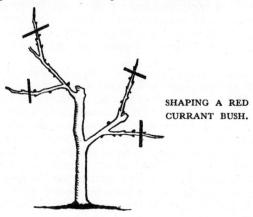

SHAPING A RED CURRANT BUSH.

Red currants may also be trained as Single or Double cordons. The single cordon is trained by cutting back all lateral growth to a single bud, growth being also pinched out during summer. The double cordon is made by cutting back the main stem to buds about 9 inches from the ground, one in either direction, the shoots being trained first at an angle of 45°, then horizontally. These shoots are tied back to wires then cut back to two buds on the upper part of the shoots, the others being rubbed out. The same procedure is given to gooseberries.

GOOSEBERRY. The removal of old wood is the most important part of pruning the gooseberry and to thin out any overcrowded growth at the centre of the tree. It is important to allow as much light as possible to reach the centre and all overcrowded growth must be cut away every winter. The gooseberry is borne on both old and new wood, but if the bush is asked to carry too much old wood, any new growth will overcrowd that already present and the fruit will eventually become very small. It is important to keep a balance between old and new wood.

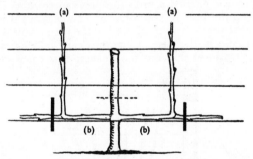

FORMING A DOUBLE CORDON. WHEN FORMED SHOOTS (*a*) HAVE THEIR LATERALS CUT BACK TO A SINGLE BUD NO OTHER GROWTH BEING ALLOWED TO FORM ON STEMS (*b*).

Where it is required to produce fruit of exhibition quality and in this the gooseberry responds well, cutting back of the new wood in summer is necessary. This is done late in July after the crop has been gathered, the fresh green shoots being pinched back to half their length. In winter they are again cut back to about 3 inches of their base. In this way the energies of the plant will be concentrated on the formation of a few fruits rather than on, perhaps, double the amount and in consequence they will make almost double the size.

Single and double cordons are formed as described for Red Currants.

Once again before doing any cutting it is important to study the habit of each variety, for some tend to form their wood in the centre of the bush, whilst others are of almost upright growth. Again, a number possess a distinct weeping habit like Whinham's Industry and where any pruning is being done the cut should always be made to an upward bud. Those with a stiff upright habit should be pruned to an outward bud, thus building up a balanced bush.

All dead wood must be removed in autumn for this may have been caused by Die Back Disease and which if not cut away might infect the whole bush.

RASPBERRIES. Here, there are two distinct times in which to prune, in early October for the summer fruiting varieties; and in early spring for those varieties that fruit in autumn. The old wood which has carried a crop the previous summer should be cut out from the base in October, the new season's wood which will bear next year's crop being tied to the wires. This is repeated each year. Also in the case of vigorous cane-making varieties it may be necessary to thin out the weakest of the new canes.

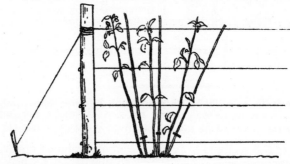

SHOWING OLD CANES WHICH SHOULD BE CUT BACK IN OCTOBER.

For autumn fruiting raspberries like November Abundance which form their fruit on the present season's wood, the canes should be cut down mid-March.

When planting new canes of either type, they should be cut

down to 3 inches of the base, preferably to a vigorous bud in early April, for it is essential for them to concentrate all their energies on the formation of new canes rather than trying to form a crop the first year and before a strong fibrous rooting system has been formed.

THE LOGANBERRY. The best time to plant is during the latter part of winter, the canes being cut back to a strong outward bud at the end of March. This will enable the plant to make vigorous cane the first summer.

For established plants, the canes which have carried the present season's crop should be cut down to their base early in autumn, and the new wood formed during the present summer is tied in to carry next year's crop. The cane of the loganberry is similar to that of the raspberry and so are many of the hybrid berries such as the Laxtonberry, Boysenberry and Youngberry, that means they are more brittle than the blackberry and its hybrids and so should be fastened to the wires in fan shape rather than horizontal position. Indeed, the loganberry contains much raspberry blood, another raspberry characteristic being its fruiting on new wood formed the previous summer.

BLACKBERRY AND HYBRIDS. Bearing their fruit both on the old wood and on the new, it is not necessary with the blackberry to cut away all old wood though several varieties are so vigorous, especially Himalaya Giant, that if the older wood is not constantly removed, the plants become a tangled mass of cane which not only makes picking most difficult but which makes training and pruning later an almost impossible task. Most blackberries should be deprived of the older canes each year and many of the vigorous shoots should be cut back in summer to keep the plants in bounds. So strong does the old wood become that a pruning saw will be required and a strong pair of gloves will be a necessity.

The late fruiting varieties Merton Thornless and John Innes are not nearly so vigorous as the other blackberries and will require the old wood removing only in alternate years. Blackberries should be pruned in early December when the leaves have fallen and one may see what is to be done without cutting away wrong canes.

When training blackberries, the canes are best tied and trained horizontally, but it is advisable to keep the old and new wood apart as far as possible, to make pruning easier. If the older wood is trained to the right and left to allow the new season's growth to be trained between, some order will be maintained. Then when the next lot of new wood is appearing, this may be trained to take the place of some of the older wood.

When planting a new blackberry, the canes should be cut back in early April to a strong bud 6 inches from the base. This will encourage the plant to make plenty of new wood which will carry a small amount of fruit the same season (autumn).

JAPANESE WINEBERRY. Neither a blackberry nor a loganberry, this makes a charming wall plant not only for its bright crimson berries which make delicious jam, but for the rich crimson colouring of its canes which are particularly warm-looking through winter. The only pruning necessary is for the occasional removing of old canes in November. The plant is equally attractive when trained up a pole or over an archway. Or, of course, it may be trained to wires in the more normal way.

INDEX

Apples, biennial cropping, 62
  branch bending, 62
  bush and standard forms, 64
  cordons, 10, 66
  dwarf pyramids, 66
  espaliers, 68
  established spur system, 58
  notching, 63, 69, 72
  pruning young trees, 54
  regulated system, 58, 60
  renewal system, 58, 61
  renovating old trees, 51
  spur bearers, 10, 59
  tip bearers, 10, 60
  varieties
    Blenheim Orange, 12, 54, 62
    Bramley's Seedling, 54, 61, 66
    Christmas Pearmain, 59
    Cox's Orange Pippin, 59
    Emneth Early, 62
    Grenadier, 62
    Lord Derby, 64
    Miller's Seedling, 62
    Newton Wonder, 54, 62
    Worcester Pearmain, 54, 67
Apricots, pruning of, 75

Bark ringing, 14, 18, 56
Blackberry, pruning of, 85
  training, 85
Black currants, 11
  pruning, 81
Brown Rot Disease, 52

Cherries, pruning of, 11, 72
  Morellos, 73
Climbing plants, 27

Die Back Disease, 84
Fig, 79
  pruning, 80
Frost and pruning, 11

Gooseberry, 81
  pruning of, 83
Gumming, of plums and cherries, 41, 42

Hedges, pruning of, 45
  arbutus, 46
  beech, 46
  box, 47
  conifers, 47
  cotoneaster, 47
  escallonia, 48
  gorse, 48
  hazel, 48
  holly, 48
  hornbeam, 48
  laurel, 48
  lonicera, 49
  olearia, 49
  pear, 49
  pittosporum, 49
  privet, 49
  pyracantha, 49
  tamarix, 50
  thuya, 50
  whitethorn, 50
  yew, 51

Japanese Wineberry, 86

Loganberry, 85

Peaches and nectarines, 73
  pruning of, 73
  training for fan shape, 74
Pears, Pitmaston Duchess, 64
  pruning of, 56
Plums, fan trained trees, 71
  pruning of, 11, 70
Pruning, correct method of, 19, 25
  necessity for, 9, 13
  results of, 12
  tools, 15

Raspberries, autumn fruiting, 14, 84
  summer fruiting, 84
Red currants, 11
  forming cordons, 83
  pruning, 82
Root pruning, 11, 13, 42, 55, 71, 80
Roses, climbers, 26, 30
  moderate pruning, 22
  pruning of 10, 20 25
  pruning standards, 23
  species, 38
  species for a hedge, 49
  suckers removal of, 25
  when to prune, 21

Saw, use of, 17
Shears, use of, 18
Shrubs, pruning of, 10, 33
  Acer, 34, 43
  Arbutus, 34
  Azalea, 34
  Berberis, 34, 47
  Buddleia, 11, 15, 34, 47
  Ceanothus, 27
  Chimonanthus fragrans, 35
  Clematis, 27
  Cornus, 35
  Coronilla glauca, 28
  Cotoneaster, 35
  Cydonia Japonica, 28
  Cytisus, 35
  Daphne, 35
  Deutzia, 35
  Elaeagnus, 28
  Forsythia, 36
  Fuchsia, 36
  Garrya elliptica, 29
  Hamamelis, 36
  Hibiscus, 36
  Honeysuckle, 29
  Hydrangea, 36, 48
  Hydrangea petiolaris, 29
  Ivy, 29
  Jasmine, 29
  Kerria, 36
  Lavender, 37
  Lilac, 11, 37

Shrubs—continued
  Magnolia, 30
  Myrtle, 30
  Osmarea, 37
  Philadelphus, 37
  Rhododendron, 37
  Ribes, 37
  Rosemary, 38
  Santolina, 38
  Senecio, 38
  Syringa, 38
  Veronica, 39
  Viburnum, 39
  Vine, ornamental, 32
  Weigela, 39
  Wisteria, 32
Silver Leaf Disease, 70, 72

Trees, Almond, 43
  Ash, 43
  Beech, 43
  Birch, 43, 47
  Cerasus, 43
  Chestnut, 43
  Conifers, 42
  Crataegus, 43
  Davidia, 44
  Elm, 44
  Hornbeam, 44
  Laburnum, 40, 44
  Lime, 44
  Mulberry, 44
  Oak, 44
  Ornamental, 39
  Poplar, 44
  Pruning, 41
  Prunus, 40, 45
  Pyrus, 45
  Renovating, 40
  Scots Pine, 40
  Silver Birch, 40
  Sorbus, 45
  Walnut, 45
  Weeping, 41
  Willow, 45

Vine, grape, 75
  Long Rod System, 76
  Outdoors, 78
  Spur System, 77

White Lead Paint, use of, 40